L♥VE AT FIRST SWIPE

A COMPREHENSIVE GUIDE TO MODERN ONLINE DATING

GARETH FOSBERRY

The stigma that was once attached to online dating has well and truly disappeared, with one in four people now finding love online.

In *Love at First Swipe*, I provide valuable tips and advice to help you navigate your way through the minefield of online dating.

There are online dating options for every type of dater and for every type of relationship preference and sexual orientation. Whether you're looking for love or for a casual relationship, there really is something out there for everyone. *Love at First Swipe* also looks at dating options for single parents, people over 50 years of age, young adults/teenagers, and people with disabilities.

Online dating has been compared to a game of cat and mouse with users constantly on the prowl, either looking for true love or looking for the "next best thing". In the fast-paced world we live in, we face many day-to-day pressures and online dating can be a welcome escape from normality. Dating apps have become a part of everyday life for many of us.

There are no set rules in the world of online dating, but there are guidelines and unwritten rules, which I will share with you in my book.

If you're wondering what to write in your profile, what profiles to avoid, where you should go on a first date, how you can tell if someone is a serial dater, should you date someone older, how do you stay safe, should you have sex on a first date, or how to tell someone that you're not interested, then this book is for you. *Love at First Swipe* will answer all of those questions and more.

Love at First Swipe also looks at modern online dating terminology, such as "catfishing" and "ghosting", plus seven of the most popular dating apps have been reviewed, so you can decide which one best matches your needs and requirements.

I also look at other factors that can help you find "The One", such as chemistry, compatibility and pheromones.

Stay safe, be honest and have respect for others. Always remain positive, as you will need a thick skin at times, but have fun and enjoy your online dating adventures.

Acorn Independent Press

CONTENTS

ABOUT THE AUTHOR: GARETH FOSBERRY

Gareth has many passions in his life, including writing, sport and music. Above all else, he values family and the power of love. Whilst sitting on a train one day, he watched people swiping left and right on their smartphones. It made him realise just how popular online dating had become, so he decided to write his own self-help book, which would delve into the world of online dating. His book draws on his own dating experiences over the past 15 years and is also based on his extensive research, with the ultimate aim of helping people.

He wanted to ensure that people avoided the common pitfalls that come with online dating, as it can be a minefield at times. It can be daunting and scary, but also fun and exciting, and it can lead to you finding happiness.

He was fascinated as to why people make the decisions they do. In any sport Gareth plays, an element of good luck is usually needed when trying to succeed. The same theory applies to online dating, as you will always need to have good luck on your side.

Gareth's book is aimed at men and woman of any age and it looks at all online dating options, whatever your relationship preference or sexual orientation. He also wanted to explore online dating options for single parents, people over 50 years old, young adults/teenagers, and people with disabilities.

Gareth would like to dedicate his book to all those people looking for love, companionship, or an open relationship. He would also like to dedicate his book to his close family and friends, especially those friends who shared their many dating stories with him, including married friends who met their partners online, which is proof that online dating can be successful.

Gareth also wants to thank Leila and Amelia at Acorn Independent Press, who helped him produce *Love At First Swipe.*

To find out more, you can visit Gareth's website at loveatfirstswipe.online or you can contact him on Twitter @garethfosberry.

1. INTRODUCTION

Around one in four relationships now start online and approximately half of all British singletons have searched for love online. These figures are thought to be even higher amongst the millennial generation. More than 50 million people in the US have also dabbled with online dating.

The world has changed so much in the past 20 years and I've seen personally how people have embraced the advance of technology over this time. The growth of the Internet, plus the increased usage of social media and online dating apps, have helped make the world a smaller place. This growth has led to more options and opportunities for us to meet new people. It also means that people can watch your every move. Your life is not as hidden or as private as it once was. In the past, you would meet someone face-to-face in a bar, at a function, at work, or through a friend or family member. Nowadays, online dating is the most popular way for people to meet.

Our smartphones have become increasingly powerful and there are now thousands of dating apps out there that you can choose from (over 7,500 at the last count). Many people do not use a desktop computer anymore when searching for anything online, as they prefer to use the smartphone in their pocket.

The stigma and negative attitude that was once attached to online dating has well and truly disappeared. In fact, it's more likely to raise eyebrows if you're single and you're *not* registered with any dating apps these days. An explosion of dating apps has taken place in recent years, simply due to the demand and popularity of the online dating market. Almost every adult in the Western world now owns a smartphone or computer.

According to eHarmony, Internet access in the UK for 18–64-year-olds has more than doubled over the past decade, and an increase in smartphone usage has helped too. You can now search for your soulmate or your next casual fling with a swipe of your finger. You have the ability to communicate with your matches at any time and from anywhere in the world. Whether you're lying in bed, drinking in a bar, sitting on a train, sunning yourself on a beach, or even taking a comfort break (but wash your hands first!), your smartphone provides you with instant access to other users.

However, more choice is not always a good thing and it can cause confusion and be overwhelming. Online dating has led to folk having less patience and people are quick to move onto the "next best thing". You could end up chatting to your neighbour, a mutual friend or a work colleague! If you're on a date, you might not be able to focus properly. Your phone might vibrate, flash brightly, or notify you that you have new messages waiting to be read when you go to the bar or go for a comfort break. One way to avoid this is to give each girl or guy that you date a fair chance – and to also keep your phone in your pocket!

Growing older can make you more choosy and that's because you are likely to be more settled in your life. You are more likely to know what you want when you're in your 30s and 40s than you did when you were in your teens and twenties. As a result of your own life experiences, you should know what you DON'T want when you reach your 30s and 40s. With age, you also become more guarded. Your barriers go up more often than they used to and with every knock you take or bad experience you have, it makes it harder to "let people in". However, being sociable with someone face-to-face on a date is completely different to "letting someone in" and taking things to the next level.

Many people struggle with commitment these days. Even if you're certain you want a relationship (with the right person), having your guard up too much can hold you back. My advice is to get to know someone well, before taking things further. If you get on well online, it's time to be brave and arrange to meet them in person, to see if you connect with each other face-to-face too.

Many singletons have said that online dating is like having a second full-time job. You come home from work after a hard day in the office, have your shower, eat your dinner, then switch on your computer or start looking at your smartphone. Before you know it, it's midnight and you've been swiping left and right for hours! Setting up an online profile is hard work. It's just like preparing your CV for a job interview, as you're trying to show yourself in the best light. Once you've registered yourself on a dating app, there's the administrative work of finding matches, sending messages and sifting through potential future partners. Then there's the synchronising of calendars when trying to arrange a date, which can prove difficult when you consider the hectic lifestyles we all lead nowadays. All of the above is a nine-to-five job in itself, and that's WITHOUT even going on the actual date. It's very easy to become addicted and burn yourself out, so the key is to go online in moderation, as well as trying to give people a fair chance.

Finding love is the most special and amazing feeling that a human will ever experience and love can be found in many forms.

> The greatest thing you'll ever learn is to love and to be loved in return.
>
> Nat King Cole

To find that special person in life, the person we want to spend the rest of our life with, is what many of us strive to achieve. However, you do need a certain amount of luck and good judgement along the way in order for that to happen.

For singletons looking for love, it has become much harder to meet people when out and about. Our lives have become busier and people don't socialise as much, so the advent of the Internet has led to online dating becoming the most popular way for people to meet. It allows complete strangers to see pictures of one another and enables them to talk to each other at the *click of a button*, or by *swiping right* on their main profile picture.

You have the ability to narrow down your search based on age, location, interests, lifestyle choices and values, meaning you can find people very quickly. If you enjoy playing tennis, jumping out of an aeroplane and singing karaoke, you'll be able to find someone with similar interests within your first hour of online dating.

The concept of swiping left or right on someone's profile is often referred to as the "swipe culture". Some say it's quite a shallow concept. In theory it is, as it's usually based solely on a person's appearance, and it can lead to a huge amount of daily rejection for someone without that person even being given a chance. But what's wrong with that? If someone swipes left on you, you will never know. If you were in a bar and you didn't like someone, you would walk straight past them, which is virtually the same as swiping left on someone's online profile and therefore rejecting them. The benefit of the swipe culture is that it lets users reject someone, guilt-free. One swipe left and it's over – no questions asked and no hurt feelings – and you can then move onto the next person. If you swipe right, it's an easy way to show you're interested, and a quick way of chatting to someone and getting to know them, before meeting them face-to-face. It's a great way to process information quickly. Simply put, online dating gives everyone more choice and enables you to narrow down your search. The swipe culture is one of the best platforms devised that allows this to happen.

I've seen and heard many people talk about the rules of online dating but, in truth, there are no set rules. However, there are guidelines and unwritten rules, which I will share with you in this book, to hopefully help you in your search. I will provide you with some useful tips and advice and talk about what you should look out for when entering the exciting, fun, yet sometimes painful minefield of online dating.

2. ONLINE DATING – QUICKER, BUT LESS PERSONAL?

We now live in a world where people communicate by e-mail, text, WhatsApp and social media, rather than talking to someone face-to-face or on the phone. Computers and smartphones have replaced handwritten communication, phone calls and simple verbal communication. Even if people are working in the same office, they often don't have the confidence, time or willingness to get up and talk to someone face-to-face. Communication through social media apps (such as Facebook, Twitter or WhatsApp) or online dating apps (such as Tinder, OkCupid, PlentyOfFish or Match.com) means that people can hide behind their phone or computer and pick and choose when they speak to someone, or when they reply to someone.

Online dating used to be something that people turned to if they had given up on the prospect of meeting someone offline. The main benefit of online dating is that you can meet people who you would never meet in your normal day-to-day life. If used in the right way, the objective of online dating is still the same as meeting someone face-to-face. This main benefit means you have greater choice and enables you to get to know people before you meet them. As long as you have the intention of actually meeting people face-to-face, then your social skills should improve, rather than worsen.

Online dating should not be viewed as a "quick fix", not when you're trying to find Mr or Ms Right. Time is needed before deciding whether to meet any potential future partner in person. You also need time to create and write your own profile, plus time to read other user's profiles too. Most importantly of all, time must be spent communicating with other users and getting to know them. Don't rush into anything! It's good to remember that the more time you spend on creating your profile, the more accurate it will be and the better your chances will be of meeting your ideal man or woman, who will make you laugh, be honest with you, have a great job, cook you meals, pamper you with gifts and be amazing in the bedroom. OK, ticking all of those boxes might be stretching it a bit!

3. THE MINEFIELD OF ONLINE DATING

Like it or not, online dating is here to stay and is becoming increasingly popular. Many people who turned their noses up at online dating sites and apps a few years ago have also now been drawn into this world, and they accept that online dating is the modern way and the easiest way to meet someone.

Online dating has become socially acceptable and this popular concept doesn't have the same stigma attached to it that it had when in its infancy. Drawing on my own experiences, I would describe online dating as being like a minefield, as there are many hazards to avoid. However, while you do need to tread carefully, the rewards can be great.

On some dating sites, such as Tinder and Bumble, you swipe right if you like someone and swipe left if you don't like them. When I say "like", it's usually that you like someone's physical appearance (normally you would just see their face in their main photo). Many users won't even bother to read a person's profile. Often, users will judge someone by their physical appearance alone, rather than by anything else – just as you would do if you saw someone in a bar, which used to be the most common way of meeting someone before online dating took hold. Of course, meeting someone online means that you don't have the physical clues – eye contact, body language, gestures and tonality – that you would have if you met someone face-to-face. And it can be a bit like a conveyor belt, as there is so much choice.

YOUR MAIN PHOTO

Your main photo is the most crucial photo that you upload onto your dating profile and it should say as much about your personality as it does about your face. Get this photo wrong and you could miss out on speaking to many potential future partners. The majority of people won't bother to look at your other photos before swiping left or right, so you should ensure that this is your BEST picture. If the same person you swiped right on also swipes right on you, you are automatically matched. This doesn't mean that you will speak to this person, though. Quite often, matches fall by the wayside because the person you matched with has so much choice and has matched with so many other people that they can pick and choose who they talk to and when they talk to them, if at all.

THE STRATEGY OF ONLINE DATING

Online dating has often been likened to a chess match. In chess, you take it in turns to manoeuvre pieces around the board. It's a very strategic game in which you have to think long and hard about your every move. Online dating is similar but, instead of making moves on a chessboard, your moves are made by sending messages back and forth, every time finding out more about each other. Any move may surprise you, so tread carefully and never dictate or predict the other person's next move.

If you are both keen to start up a conversation, the messages should flow and you will begin the process of getting to know that person. However, no matter how much you find out about each other and how well you get on with someone online, this does not guarantee that you will both connect, if and when you meet up in person.

There are still so many unanswered questions. Are their photos recent? Are their photos really of them? Are they really who they say they are? What are they really looking for? Often, people fabricate the truth and, with so much choice nowadays, a lot of users simply just want fun. It can be a personal competition for some users as to how many notches they can get on the bedpost.

Many users don't talk to their date on the phone before they actually meet them in person, so not hitting it off could come down to something as simple as not liking their accent when you get together. You might not understand what your date is saying because of a different dialect or a language barrier. They may even have an undeclared disability. Perhaps you would have known more about each other had you both spoken on the phone before you met in person.

There will be people you talk to online who are just looking for a casual relationship. They might tell you that they're looking for a long-term relationship when in fact they're not. If they're not lying to you, they may be confused about what they want. This could be a reason why someone has been single for a long time. Also, they might be so caught up in the world of online dating that they regularly go online because they're addicted. It might also be for no other reason than through sheer boredom. You should be wary of the "serial dater", which I will talk more about later. I've also heard online dating being described as "disposable", as you can move on to the next person far too quickly and therefore don't invest enough time in the first person you speak to. Too much choice can confuse the way you think and also overwhelm you.

Meeting someone online can also lower your inhibitions as people naturally feel safer and more anonymous talking to someone online. There is less at stake when chatting online and you are distanced from the impact of your words. As a result, you might say or write things to a new online connection that you would not say to someone face-to-face.

4. SAFETY & SECURITY FIRST (!)

Ensuring you have strong security settings is imperative in everything you do online, as there are people who would take advantage if they knew too much about you.

Online dating is an exciting place to be, but it can also be a scary place. I cannot emphasise enough how important it is to take safety precautions. Never put your personal safety or your privacy at risk. Don't give away too much personal information on your profile page, especially not your phone number or your e-mail address, which could easily fall into the wrong hands. If you want to swap numbers with someone that you like, that's fine, but be selective and certainly don't do it straight away. Also, don't accept a Facebook friend request from someone until you've met them in person and know more about them.

> Your online profile stated you were tall, dark and handsome. Have you considered a career in fiction writing?

Many dating apps, such as Tinder and Zoosk, let their users sync their profile with their Facebook account, but not all mobile daters want their family, friends and the rest of the world to know they are searching for love online. Privacy filters allow you to specify how much of your information is visible to other users, but your profile picture is still visible to everyone.

The online dating website or app you are using will have built-in security features that you can choose to take advantage of. You also have the ability to block someone from contacting you and to report someone if they are being a nuisance. In addition, many dating sites feature the ability to turn off notifications, instant messages, location tracking, etc. As soon as you have signed up, you should check the privacy settings page on your dating website or app to see what features are available.

It's good to be cautious and wary, as most online dating sites don't conduct background checks or verify information. You may come across people with criminal records, married people and people who may be mentally unstable.

It's always best to let a friend or family member know when and where you are going on a date and who you are going on the date with, especially if you're a woman. On a first date, never agree to let your date pick you up from your home or from your workplace, as they would then already know too much about you! You don't know this person and you would be taking a huge risk with your safety and security. Always meet your date in a public place where you will feel safe, and don't tell them where you live or work, or reveal any information about your personal finances.

THREE TOP TIPS

1) Do NOT send money or talk about your finances to anyone you meet online – for any reason. If your online connection asks for money, you should treat this as a scam. There are lots of smooth talkers who are swindlers that want to steal your hard-earned cash. Don't let them!
2) Take great caution when posting photos. Do not post photos with your home or workplace in the background, nor pictures of your children or anyone else's children. Check your pictures before you post them.
3) Do not send any naked pictures to anyone you haven't met, as you don't know what they will do with them. Once you have sent them, you lose control of them and they could end up anywhere.

4. SAFETY & SECURITY FIRST (!)

These are enough reasons to show why it's best to first get to know someone well before you meet them and why you shouldn't give out too much information. Especially, don't give out any personal information, such as where you live and work, your contact details, information about your children/people you know, or your bank details.

5. SCAMMERS, SOB STORIES & SCAM-PACKS

We've all had a scammer contact us at some point, right? Whether it be an e-mail at work from someone in Africa or South America asking us for money, a phone call from a person trying to sell us double glazing, where there ends up being lots of "extras", or an online dating message from someone telling us how handsome or pretty we are and declaring their undying love for us!

Scammers who contact you through an online dating app will often tell you a sob story to make you feel sorry for them. Their sob story usually gets told within your first few message exchanges. They'll say they've lost a family member in a tragic way, or that they have a family member with a terrible illness. They'll say they need money to help them pay for medical care or travel costs. THIS IS A SCAM!

Scammers may also take on a false identity. There are examples of scammers pretending to be an old school friend that you haven't seen for years. They'll say they always liked you when you were younger and that they would like to meet you again now, romantically, but they need you to pay their travel costs so they can come and see you. Often, these people don't have any photos on their profile. THIS IS A SCAM!

Sometimes a scammer will have just one photo posted and, unsurprisingly, they will look like a model! Don't be fooled! You can do an image search of your admirer to help determine if they really are who they say they are. You can use image search services on Google or TinEye.

Unbelievably, criminals can now purchase "scam packs" on the dark web, containing love letter templates, photos, videos and false identities, for as little as a few dollars. So many people fall for the scams that the price of these packs has dropped, due to the high volume being sold as the demand is so great. Often, the scammer's messages are missing words and the grammar they use isn't great. It's common for them to say, "Hello dear" or "I think you could be the love of my life" or "I need money to help pay for..." blah blah blah! Don't be fooled!

Other than bad spelling and grammar mistakes, you need to be aware of inconsistencies in their stories and other signs that you're being scammed, such as their camera never working if you've asked them to use Skype. Just to reiterate again, you need to be cautious when sharing personal photos or videos with prospective partners, especially naked photos, or photos with your children, residence or workplace in the background. Scammers are known to blackmail their targets using compromising material and they can use your photos/videos against you, with the main aim being to swindle more money from your bank account.

You must NEVER give your bank details to anyone or transfer any money into anyone's bank account. These are complete strangers. You have never met them. They prey on people's fantasies and their desperation to find someone to love. If you come across similar situations, you should block these people and also report them to the helpdesk on your dating app of choice.

One important issue that online dating sites and apps need to improve on is their "vetting process". More needs to be done – and could be done – to stop scammers from creating online dating profiles.

In a recent study of nine online dating apps by Kaspersky Internet Security, their researchers discovered that four of the nine they investigated allowed potential criminals to work out who was hiding behind a nickname, based on data provided by the users themselves. For example, Tinder, Happn and Bumble let anyone see a user's specified place of work or study. Using this information, it's possible for scammers to find the user's social media accounts and discover their real names. BE CAREFUL HOW MUCH INFORMATION YOU PUT ON YOUR PROFILE.

If someone wants to know your location, six of the nine apps studied will lend a hand. Only OkCupid, Bumble and Badoo keep user location data under lock and key. All of the other apps indicate the distance between you and the person you're chatting to. By moving around and logging data about the distance between the two of you, it's easy for any scammer or complete WEIRDO to determine a very close location of the "prey" – YOU!! You can usually turn your location tracking/GPS on and off quite easily, so you might not want to keep this on all of the time – just turn it on when you're actually online looking for people within a certain radius.

If you have provided your account details to a scammer, or sent money to them, contact your bank or financial institution immediately. You should also contact the police and report the scammer to your dating app of choice.

6. WHAT DO I WRITE IN MY PROFILE?

Constructing your profile takes time and you want to get this right. Not every dating site puts the emphasis on pictures alone; some focus more on what you put in your profile, so you can find your "compatible matches". On some dating sites, such as eHarmony and OkCupid, they ask you to complete their compatibility questionnaire and, based on your answers, you're matched with people who have similar interests, personality traits and values as yourself, and with people who you are physically compatible with.

In a recent survey by eHarmony, they identified the five most attractive words that men and women put down in their profile. These are the **five most attractive words** identified:

Five words men should consider putting in their online dating profile
1. Physically fit (+96% more interaction than daters who did not use this)
2. Perceptive (+51%)
3. Spontaneous (+45%)
4. Outgoing (+44%)
5. Optimistic (+39%)

Five words women should consider putting in their online dating profile
1. Ambitious (+48%)
2. Perceptive (+46%)
3. Sweet (+33%)
4. Hard-working (+32%)
5. Thoughtful (+28%)

Creating your profile is usually the hardest part when registering yourself on a dating site, but it's also the most important part. Make sure you tell the truth and use words that reflect positivity. There's no point in lying or using false pictures as you won't be successful, your date will feel deceived and you will just be cheating yourself. If someone likes you, they have to like you for who you really are.

UPLOADING PHOTOS

Make sure you upload recent photos, not photos of you from 10 years ago! Also, make sure your pictures show you in a good light, and use filters, if necessary. You should be smiling and not looking miserable! You should include photos of yourself that are flattering. Uploading colourful, varied and fun profile photos is essential to creating a great online dating profile. Make sure you include photos that are representative of who you are. Upload photos of you glammed up, dressed down, resting and letting your hair down. Use photos where you are smiling or having fun. You want to project yourself as someone who is multidimensional and uploading photos such as these to your profile will reflect this.

DON'T LIE ABOUT YOURSELF

Lying about yourself isn't a good basis on which to start any relationship. If you're looking to settle down and start a family, or if you've already started a family, say so. Be honest about your age, height, weight and what you're looking for. If anything serious develops with this person they'll find out the truth anyway, so it's always better to be upfront and not lie or deceive. If you can't be honest about what you want and who you are at this stage, how can you expect to find someone who likes you for being you and expect any relationship to last? The truth will always come out in the end.

WORDING AND TRAITS YOU CAN USE ON YOUR PROFILE

Even if you write that you enjoy "lying on a beach in the sun" or that you like "going to nice bars and restaurants", you should maybe think of adding more to these statements, as everyone says those things. Think of something interesting that you could add, such as where this beach would be and what drink you would be sipping on the beach or what type of restaurants you like and your favourite foods.

You could list any hobbies you have and/or any sports or gym activities that you like playing or participating in. People need to imagine how they would fit into your life, so you should give them enough information to make them want to know more about you.

Everyone looks for somebody who has good character. Your profile could mention family and friends, volunteering and enjoying spending time with children, or it could describe your most prominent and positive character traits. Are you funny, caring, outgoing, creative, loyal or affectionate? These are all great traits that people always look for when swiping right for love.

You can also include information about what you care about and what you're passionate about. This could be sport, music, arts and crafts, travelling, helping others, volunteer work, playing poker, rescuing stray dogs, learning new languages, or writing. The right person will like what they read and will be interested in finding out more about you.

7. WHAT DO I LOOK FOR IN AN IDEAL PARTNER?

With online dating, many people are attracted to someone's photos initially, rather than by what they've written in their profile – if they've actually written anything at all.

If a person hasn't written anything in their profile, this should be a "warning sign", but it shouldn't necessarily mean you avoid them completely. However, I would question whether they are taking it seriously, or whether the reason they cannot be bothered to write anything is because they are serial daters who are just looking for fun, so it does depend on what you're looking for yourself.

If you've found a match, most women like a man to show an interest in them, so if you're a man, seize the initiative and send a message to the woman first. It's at this stage that the questions will begin and you start to find out more about someone.

Being caring and funny are traits that people usually look for, plus, a woman likes a man who shows a keen interest in her and asks her questions.

If you get on well for a period of time, you would usually swap phone numbers and arrange to meet up. Just don't ask for someone's phone number straight away, as this happens often and usually scares a woman off (it can scare a man off too!).

The next stage is to take the plunge and meet your match face-to-face.

8. SWIPING RIGHT FOR LOVE

You may have been "ghosted" in the past, after a first date which, in your mind, went well. "Ghosting" means that you never hear from that person again. Having an experience like this makes it more difficult to imagine ever having a successful second date, let alone a third.

Online dating can be frustrating and everyone has had bad experiences, but your future partner could be out there waiting for you to both swipe right on each other, so you should never give up.

Many people searching for love have a few different dating apps uploaded onto their phone. This is usually an attempt to create more options, in the belief that the more people they chat to, the more chances they have of meeting Mr or Ms Right. Even with all those apps and all those choices at your fingertips, you could still be single. Instead of spending all your money, time and energy on every app under the sun, just choose one that actually works well for you and concentrate your efforts on that one app. Don't be too greedy, as it's not healthy.

Several right swipes and lots of matches in a row might give you an ego boost and put a smile on your face, but the huge choice you have won't help you find an honest, supportive, dependable, loyal partner – if that's what you're really looking for. Don't get confused and swipe right just based on looks. Take your time to analyse photos and read people's profiles, to figure out if the match could actually be the right person for you.

It often happens that you spend ages chatting to someone but they don't ask you out and they're just happy to chat. They don't even want to go for a coffee. So it's frustrating when you realise you've just been wasting your time.

If you're always the first to message and a pattern is forming, this is not right. I don't mind texting someone first, but I certainly won't text first all the time. It's a question of pride. If they never miss you or they don't think enough of you to want to see how you're doing by initiating contact or if you're always the one doing the calling or texting, there's a high chance that they will eventually cease communication completely and there'll be nothing you can do about it.

Secondly, you should ask yourself if your communication is always sexual. You may tell them that you're off to see a show with friends, or that you're having a busy day at work. If the conversation somehow takes on a sexual theme most of the time, that's a clear sign that they don't really care about you and they're just looking for you to boost their ego and give them what they desire sexually, but once they've had their fill, they will disappear.

Despite such frustrations, the popularity of dating apps has grown relentlessly in recent years. According to app research firm, App Annie, in 2016, around £234m was spent on dating apps. This nearly doubled to £448m in 2017.

In 2017, dating apps accounted for three of the top 10 apps by consumer spend in the UK. Whilst in France, they accounted for six of the top 10 apps by consumer spend! This is exactly why dating app designers are constantly coming up with new ways of keeping users engaged. (Source: Paul Barnes, a director at App Annie.)

New research carried out by Match.com has revealed that the average cost of a date in the UK is a rather astounding £129, across both people, which makes Brits the biggest investors in dating in Europe by a long way. The next biggest spenders on dates are the Spanish, at £55, followed by the Dutch, at £52.

9. HOW SOON SHOULD I MEET SOMEONE & WILL I BE SAFE?

Whilst it's good not to become pen pals by talking to someone for months on end before going on a date, it's wise **not** to meet someone immediately, no matter how much you think you like them.

When we were children, our mothers and our teachers at school would always say, "Don't talk to strangers" as a stranger could cause us harm. This same warning can be applied to online dating. Yes, you have to "talk" to people online in the first instance, but you should still heed the main point of the message, which is that it can be dangerous when meeting a stranger, even if you have chatted to them online for a while.

BUILD UP SOME SORT OF CONNECTION AND RELATIONSHIP FIRST

If you're constantly contacting someone first or you're the only one asking the questions, the probability is that they're really not that interested in you. The key is to build up some sort of connection and relationship with them first, before you meet them face-to-face. Don't make exceptions, no matter how much you like someone physically from their photos, as this often does not work out.

If someone asks to meet you straight away without you knowing anything about them, the alarm bells in your head should start ringing. Don't do it!!

If you meet someone in person immediately, it's a huge safety and security risk. You should ask yourself, "How many other people are they asking to meet immediately?" and "Are they going on multiple dates every week?". That would really turn me off! You should want someone to show a keen interest in you first before you meet them so at least there's some sort of connection, otherwise you could be wasting your time, energy and money, as it could go horribly wrong and things could feel really awkward on your date.

I have met people very quickly in the past and found that we didn't click at all and had nothing in common. I felt like I'd rather be anywhere else than there with them!

Someone in person can be completely different to the person you've been chatting to online. For all you know, they could be a psychopath or an axe murderer! It's always better – and safer – to see as many pictures of someone as you can, to make sure it is definitely them (although you can never be 100% sure). Find out as much as possible about them first, for safety and security reasons more than anything else. **Always meet in a public place on the first date.** Your date might look and sound like a completely different person when you meet them face-to-face.

If someone's opening line is, "What are your thoughts on getting to know someone in person, rather than via text?" without engaging in any conversation first, they clearly don't want to hang around and waste any time! Whilst it's good to eventually meet someone face-to-face, don't waste your time when you don't have a connection and don't know anything about them. I appreciate that you're not going to connect with everyone you meet in person, even if you get on well online, but you should find out more about them first. You should know where they live, what they do for a living, if they have been single long, if they have any children, what they do in their spare time and what they are looking for. You might have absolutely nothing in common with them whatsoever, so it's a huge risk meeting someone immediately when you don't know anything about them.

Get to know someone well first. See if they show an interest in you and see whether you have things in common.

10. PEN PALS & THE "FRIEND ZONE"

The main purpose of online dating is to date people and, ultimately, to find your perfect match, so you shouldn't be on a dating site if you're just looking for a pen pal.

If your match hasn't asked you out on a date after an extended period of messaging, they might not be interested in actually dating. They could be bored and looking for a way to kill some time. You could be the one to make the first move and suggest meeting up in person, but if they find an excuse not to take you up on your offer, it's not a good sign. I would usually give someone one chance, but if they found another excuse, it's time to move on!

Make sure you don't fall into the dreaded "friend zone". Keep all conversation light and complimentary and show a keen interest in that person by asking questions regularly.

Try to avoid your conversation becoming overtly sexual or you could end up with an unwarranted naked picture from an escaped convict! You might think you know someone from chatting online for a while, but you could be in for a nasty surprise. If someone doesn't reciprocate and ask you questions as well, they're clearly not interested in you, but if they do and you've built up a nice connection, it's time to meet up, otherwise you could be dumped in the friend zone.

Some users are looking for a quick fix, so conversations of a sexual nature are commonplace. Try to avoid sexting with someone that you've just started chatting with and hardly know. They might not be interested in meeting you at all and you could end up being ghosted or falling into the friend zone.

You won't have a romantic connection with everyone you date, so the doors to the friend zone are also open to the people who you get on really well with, just not romantically, for whatever reason. You might still want to keep in touch with each other and it's possible that you become friends instead. I have made friends with some people I've dated in the past, where we get on really well, just not romantically.

11. WHAT PROFILES YOU SHOULD AVOID & WHAT NOT TO PUT ON YOUR OWN PROFILE

Some popular dating apps, such as Tinder and Bumble, have been devised so that potential matches are chosen based on their looks, rather than what's written in their profile, but there is still a small space for you to write about yourself and tell everyone what you're looking for. Other dating apps, such as eHarmony and OkCupid, allow you to write much more about yourself. They also ask you specific questions, using their compatibility questionnaire. Many users upload photos or write a description about themselves that do them no favours whatsoever, so next we have 10 things that you should be wary of when looking at or reading someone's profile (you should also avoid putting anything similar on your own profile).

1) TOPLESS OR HALF-NAKED PICTURES
Usually, this person is only after a casual relationship. While it's clear they are very confident about how they look, it's likely they're an arrogant person. They are superficial and spend more time focusing on their muscles or cleavage rather than developing other parts of their personality. They are obsessed with physical appearance and it will be hard for them to find someone that measures up. They aren't serious about online dating – or, at least, they're not looking for anything serious.

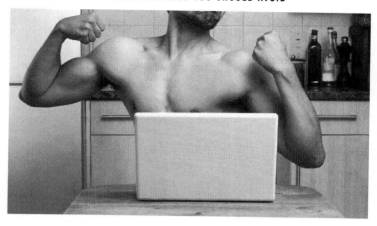

2) PEOPLE WHO CAN'T SPELL AND USE POOR GRAMMAR

Aside from giving a bad first impression, many online daters list spelling mistakes and poor grammar as being among their pet hates. Good spelling and grammar show that you took care and attention before saving your description to your profile. Bad spelling and grammar can also come across as lazy, as most dating sites have a spellcheck option.

3) PEOPLE WITH NO PHOTOS

Don't even think about creating your dating profile without posting a photo. A pictureless profile says that you are shy or insecure or, maybe, both. Other users will think, "What is wrong with them?", "Are they married?", "They are so lazy!" or "Have they just escaped from prison?". It's best to avoid anyone who has not uploaded a photo, as they could be a scammer.

4) PEOPLE WITH ONLY ONE PHOTO

Everyone who likes your main photo will want to see more, not because they can't get enough of you, but because a single photo is not a reliable indicator of what you look like. There are many frauds out there who steal a photo from the Internet or from someone else. Usually it's a photo of someone more attractive than them. The person using someone else's photo is known as a "Catfish". You should upload a minimum of three photos.

If someone doesn't have a photo, or they only have one photo on their profile, it's likely that they're not that serious about meeting someone, that they already have a partner, or that they're hiding something. However, research has shown there is a difference between a man and a woman who only has one picture posted. When a woman posts one picture it's usually for safety reasons.

5) PEOPLE WITH PHOTOS FROM THE SHOULDERS UP ONLY

You should ask yourself, "What are they hiding?". You might like their face, but will you like the rest of their physical appearance? You should naturally be a little wary of people without any full-length photos. A full-length photo will give you a clearer picture of the person you are chatting to. It also means you'll not have any nasty surprises when you meet them in person.

6) PEOPLE WITH A WISH LIST OF THE EXACT PERSON THEY'RE LOOKING FOR

Some online dating profiles read like a shopping list. If a user is looking for someone with blue eyes, blond hair, between 5 feet 10 inches and 6 feet tall, from Manchester, etc., this should immediately put anyone off. A detailed list like this makes the user sound like a control freak and their requirements could be an exact description of their ex!

7) PEOPLE WITH NOTHING WRITTEN IN THEIR PROFILE

It is difficult to interact with someone who has nothing in their profile. They might be worried about giving out too much information about themselves for security reasons, or they might not be that bothered and just seeing what all the fuss is about. They may also be new to online dating and not had the time to write their profile yet. It's always best to chat to someone who has something in their profile though, as they are less likely to be hiding something and you can see if you have things in common.

8) PEOPLE WHO ASK YOU LOTS OF PERSONAL QUESTIONS, BUT YOU DON'T FIND OUT ANYTHING ABOUT THEM

They could be a scammer or a catfish and they might only be after your money. Don't give away too much information and don't meet anyone without seeing several photos of them first. If they add you as a friend on Facebook, don't accept their friend request.

9) SOMEONE PHOTOGRAPHED NEXT TO A TIGER OR A LION

This person is deluded. They think that posting a photo of them up close and personal with a big cat will vastly increase their sex appeal and desirability to other singletons. How can people sense you are a potential lover if you put up a tiger-selfie?? The general idea is that women love travel and danger, so if a man wants to attract a girl, all he has to do is demonstrate this in his profile picture. This user feels that uploading a photo of themselves with a big cat is the best way to do this!

10) SOMEONE WHO SAYS ON THEIR PROFILE, "I HAVE JUST COME OUT OF A LONG-TERM RELATIONSHIP"

To mention this in their profile means they are possibly still hurting and might not be over their recent split. You should tread carefully if you are dating anyone who is on the rebound and/or has very recently come out of a long-term relationship, as their emotions might be all over the place. You should also avoid people who have uploaded a photo showing them standing next to their ex.

12. FIRST IMPRESSIONS

It has often been said that the first five minutes you spend with someone will tell you more about them than anything you'll learn about them over the months and years to come.

With online dating, most communication happens on a non-verbal level at the start. This means that sensory factors – such as how we look, what we sound like and how we smell, which drive many of the impressions that are conveyed when we meet someone new – aren't yet available to us.

You only get one chance to make a good first impression. Not only will you be judged on your appearance, but also on your attitude and personality. You should feel excitement at the prospect of meeting your date for the first time. Of course, feeling nervous is perfectly normal too, as both these feelings go hand-in-hand.

In this modern age of online dating, it's more nerve-racking than ever before to meet someone in person for the first time. Hopes and dreams are created through the initial conversations you have online. Your expectations are higher than if you met someone in a bar, as you already have a virtual connection with that person, albeit not a physical one.

You may suffer disappointment should your date turn out to be different from the preconceived image you had formed in your mind. That being said, the person you meet can sometimes exceed your expectations, or they can grow on you over time, and vice-versa. It's best not to look too far ahead before you meet your date in person. That way, if you do suffer disappointment, it's not something that you will dwell on for too long.

Make sure the first impression you give is a great one. A first impression is made within the first seven seconds of meeting someone new. When you meet someone for the first time, your date will be making a rapid inventory of your build, smell, height, smile, eye contact, handshake, kiss, confidence and how you present yourself. You will also be making your own inventory of them.

One golden rule is to practise **good hygiene**. Whilst looks aren't everything, both men and women are often impressed by a person who appears to take pride in their appearance and who looks after themselves. Make sure you are clean, that you wear your favourite clothes or outfit (but don't look scruffy), splash on your favourite perfume or aftershave, smile often, keep good posture, make good eye contact with your date and keep your body relaxed. **Be kind** to your date as well, and don't treat them badly. Whether you end up liking each other or not, you've both invested a lot of time and energy into preparing for your date, so don't be rude and don't disappear on them.

Most important of all, **be yourself**. Yes, of course you have to make a big effort and you could be very nervous, but try to relax and show your date what you are really like as a person.

13. WHERE DO YOU GO ON A FIRST DATE & WHO PAYS?

These are two common questions to which there are no right or wrong answers. As the Boy Scout motto advises, "Be prepared", and make sure you have a plan in advance. If you are arranging the first date, let your date know the idea you have in mind, along with the venue and location you have decided on. Ask your date if they are happy with your idea and with your choice of venue and location. Make sure they are happy and comfortable with everything.

If you're an old-fashioned male, you would tend to pay for drinks and/or dinner on the first date. It has long been commonplace for a man to pay on the first date if they have made the arrangements regarding where you go. However, we now live in a much more equal world and your date might want to pay their way.

Meeting different people is very common these days and it can mean an expensive outlay, especially if you have several first dates over a short period of time.

I often used to go for a meal on a first date and would pay the entire bill. I soon realised this was not a good idea when I ran into financial difficulties. Nowadays, I tend to go for drinks on a first date. Aside from the financial aspect, you might not like or connect with that person in real life, even though you got on really well when you chatted online. By going for a drink, it also means you can "politely" make a sharp exit if things aren't going so well. Just don't jump out of a toilet window as it can be very painful if you fall – and embarrassing too!

If things do go well on a first date, a second date is on the cards. If you start dating someone regularly, the question of "who pays?" will be a regular thought. If you both work, then it's quite fair for you to have a chat beforehand and agree to "go Dutch" on the bill. That means you split the final bill and pay half each. Society has changed and there are more women in the workforce than ever before. However, you need to be considerate. If your date works part-time to accommodate family commitments, they won't be on an equal footing with anyone who works full-time, especially since many part-time jobs tend to be poorly paid. Plenty of couples go Dutch or figure out other ways to equally share the weight of anything finance-related.

If a woman offers to pay half of the bill or offers to buy alternate rounds of drinks, that says to me they are unselfish and have a caring nature. It tells me a lot about them as a person, although I would still insist on paying on the majority of occasions, especially on a first date, as I think a man should do this. It's a very delicate subject that's not often spoken about, but it's a question that everyone has to deal with on a regular basis.

Some people go to the cinema on a first date. Although it can be fun watching a movie together, it doesn't allow you to talk and get to know someone, which is ideally what you want to do on a first date. Also, you might not feel a connection with someone in person, so you might never see them again. If you're paying, it would be a waste of money – especially if the film isn't good!

One genuine comment which a user wrote on their profile definitely shows they know what they want (which is a positive), but it can also be perceived as them being demanding (which is a negative), so make your own mind up: "Don't ask me out for coffee or drinks, it's just an insult! Traditional dinner and telephone calls only!" If you're in a position where money is tight, or you don't agree with paying for everything on a first date, or maybe you don't like using the phone to talk to people initially, it's probably a wise idea to avoid speaking to someone like this.

14. COMPATIBILITY & CHEMISTRY

When you have chemistry with someone, it's a **natural** feeling and attraction. It's also a **mutual** feeling and attraction. You won't have chemistry with everyone though, so someone that you're attracted to might not be to somebody else's taste. Finding great chemistry is rare. When you're dating someone that you're not compatible with it's fairly obvious, and you usually find this out pretty quickly. Most online dating books and apps tend to gloss over the important concepts of compatibility and chemistry.

Compatibility and chemistry will come naturally and cannot be faked or changed. With all the extra pressures we face in the world today, we often try to be someone we're not. This is in an attempt to impress people and promote ourselves by increasing the romantic and sexual signals that we give off to potential partners. Dating advice is designed to help us find the man or woman of our dreams, or to find someone we feel is out of our league, to try and get them to notice us, the type of person you've never had before, or the person that you've fantasised about. Yet, if you're not compatible with this particular guy or girl, it won't lead to anything.

Compatibility and chemistry do not have the same meaning, yet people often think they do. Chemistry is a word that people use loosely to define a connection that exists in the invisible space between two people. It is an unspoken and unseen connection, or the lack of it, sometimes.

Compatibility is where you both have similar morals, values, beliefs and lifestyle choices. For example, if monogamy is important to you, then you won't be compatible with someone who is looking for a casual relationship. If you enjoy going down the gym and being active and your date is a couch potato, then again, you will not be compatible.

It is important to also note that love and compatibility are not the same thing, although they are very often confused for one another. Even if you are intensely attracted to someone, this doesn't always translate to a thriving relationship with that person.

Chemistry represents the emotional connection present when you're both around each other. Two people who have a high degree of chemistry have emotional make-ups and personalities that bring out the best in each other and make one another feel warm inside. This creates a constant positivity between you, and you will continue to make each other feel happy. When you have a high degree of chemistry with someone, they take over your thoughts and your time. You will be excited at the thought of talking to them and seeing that person again. You'll hope that every call or text is him/her and you will constantly wonder what your partner thinks about something. It is often referred to as "having butterflies", which is the excitement you feel and which can lead to love.

It is harder to identify specific examples of what creates strong chemistry, but it could be the way you laugh at each other's jokes, the attentiveness you show each other, asking questions about each other's day, good surprises you may spring on one another when you/they least expect it, such as ordering flowers, the way you hold each other's hand in public, the way you kiss or hug each other, or it could be a willingness to help with a project, such as decorating a new house.

Chemistry is made up of subtle and continuous behaviours and dispositions that create positivity and warm feelings with the other person. Chemistry should be felt immediately if it's there and felt by both parties equally. If you don't feel this, then there's a problem. The most important rule about chemistry is that, whatever you're feeling, your partner will pick up on those feelings. They are also likely to have the same feelings as you, which means that you are very similar to one another and are therefore an ideal match!

15. TOP 10 UNWRITTEN RULES OF ONLINE DATING

Dating can be very tricky and there are lots of questions that you need to consider when meeting someone for the first time. Where should you meet? What clothes/aftershave/perfume should you wear? Do you drive or do you take public transport? Do you drink alcohol? What do you talk about? Who should pay? How soon after your date should you message or call them? So many questions spin around your head before, during and after a date, which is why I've compiled this list of the top 10 unwritten rules for dating, to help make sure your date is a success.

1) MAKE SURE YOU MEET YOUR DATE IN A PUBLIC PLACE WHERE YOU'LL BOTH FEEL COMFORTABLE

Safety and security are extremely important and you want to make your date feel comfortable right from the start. If you're a man, you might think that you're being a gentleman if you let your date decide where you go on your first date, but women often like to see a man take control. In addition to safety and security, dating can be a daunting experience, so these are all reasons why you should help cut through the nerves by arranging to meet up in familiar territory and in a public place. This will help make you both feel more comfortable. Maybe avoid your regular bar, pub or restaurant, as bumping into your friends on a first date could be a little distracting and can also make things awkward between you and your date.

2) FIRST IMPRESSIONS ARE ALWAYS IMPORTANT

First impressions are lasting impressions. They are so important and, if you get this right, it will set the tone not just for the night, but also for any future relationship you may have with that person. You may have lucky clothes that you always wear, but if they are ripped, scruffy or dirty, this will be the first impression your date gets of you. You should never pretend to be someone that you're not, but equally, your date might like to see that you take pride in your appearance. This doesn't necessarily mean you have to wear a dress, suit or tuxedo, but looking smart, smelling nice and being clean (don't turn up with dirty fingernails!) will help you impress your date and get you off to a good start, without you falling at the first hurdle or having to play catch-up. You should be yourself in terms of what you wear, but you should make an effort and look smart. You also need to make sure you turn up to your date on time, as there will be a black mark put against you if you don't.

Leading on from your initial conversations online, it's now all about finding out whether you have a physical, emotional, mental and intellectual connection and the only way to find this out is by meeting someone face-to-face.

3) GET THE SEATING ARRANGEMENTS RIGHT

If you're a man, you should always let the woman sit down first. Pull out the chair for her if you can. In one-on-one situations, etiquette suggests that the lady is offered the seat with the view into the room and the gentleman takes the seat facing the wall. This is so the lady gets the nicer view and will be the one who is looking out into the bar, pub or restaurant. You would then be looking at her, with the wall behind her.

The seat facing the wall will often back on to an aisle. It's, therefore, more likely to get bumped into, which is another reason why the man should sit there. Furthermore, someone could spill something as they're walking past, so the man should be protective of his date and should be the one risking hot food falling onto his lap or a glass of wine being spilt down his back.

4) BE CONFIDENT, BUT NOT ARROGANT

Confidence in a man or woman can be a very attractive trait. Most people see confidence as an important factor when it comes to choosing a partner. Even if you're a little shy, you can practice beforehand by talking to someone you know. Of course, the more dates you go on, the more experience you gain and the more confident you should naturally become. Plan what you are going to talk about on your date, including subjects that you're enthusiastic about, such as any hobbies you have or sports you participate in.

You should find out as much information as you can about your date before you meet them face-to-face, as it's even better if you have mutual interests that you can talk about. Many people are shy and worry terribly about their appearance. It's more attractive if your date sees that you're comfortable in your own skin and are happy being you.

There is a fine line between confidence and arrogance though. The last thing your date wants to hear is you bragging and talking about yourself all night! Try to keep the conversation flowing, but make sure you ask questions and compliment your date as well.

5) DON'T DO ALL THE TALKING AND DO ASK QUESTIONS

Make sure you don't do all the talking on your date! It's good to talk about yourself, as you're both finding out more about each other, but make sure you also ask your date questions, as it shows that you're interested in what they have to say and that you're a good listener.

You don't want your date to start yawning or looking at their watch, so keep them on their toes by asking questions. Don't be scared of pauses in conversation – if you like each other you should feel comfortable with natural pauses in conversation.

6) KEEP THE CONVERSATION FUN

It is essential on your first date to try and avoid any negative, in-depth conversations, such as why you don't enjoy your job, any bad dating experiences you've had, money problems, or any other issues you might have been having. Keep the conversation light-hearted and talk about fun experiences you've had. Try and sprinkle some humour into your conversation as well. Both women and men want someone who can make them laugh and who has a good sense of humour. You do have to be serious at times, but in the early stages of dating, don't forget to have some fun!

7) TRY TO AVOID TALKING ABOUT EXES

Most of us have a history of exes. We've all had personal issues and relationship problems that we've had to deal with in the past, but it's best to never admit anything to a new or potential lover on the first date. Your date knows you have a past, but they usually don't want to hear about it. Keep away from the "ex" conversation until you know each other better. It will inevitably come up in conversation in time, but as a general rule, it's best to stay away from the subject altogether on a first date if you can. Your date does not usually want to hear about your ex and it can make things feel awkward between you. If your date brings up the subject, it's best to try and keep answers short (without appearing suspicious). If needed, reassure your date that your past is history and that you want to spend your time getting to know them instead. If your date talks a lot about an ex, it's likely they are on the rebound and haven't got over a recent split. This is not a good sign! It's usually best to avoid dating someone who has only recently come out of a long-term relationship as their head may be all over the place and their feelings could still be very raw.

8) TURN OFF YOUR PHONE

It can be very annoying and irritating if a phone starts ringing in the middle of your date and it's rude if you answer it in front of the person you are with. There may be a genuine reason to have your phone switched on, but at least make sure you have it on silent or on vibrate. If you need to check it, you should do this when you go to the bar or for a comfort break. If you check it in front of your date, it says to them that you're not interested in them and that you are not focusing entirely on your date. It would be very rude and disrespectful. They will appreciate it more if you take the time to engage with them fully.

9) OFFER TO PAY

This is a really sensitive subject and there is no right or wrong answer to the question of "who pays?"

On the first date, the man often treats the woman, especially if he has arranged the date. However, times have changed and the man should not be too forceful if the woman insists on paying her way; this will make him look like a gentleman in the woman's eyes. If the woman wants to pay her share, the man could suggest she gets the bill on the next date, if she wishes. That's IF there is a next date! If the date isn't going well and you know you won't see each other again, it's probably best to just "go Dutch" and split the bill.

10) CHECK ON YOUR DATE TO MAKE SURE THEY GOT HOME SAFELY

If you don't want a second date, it's best to be honest about it. Don't say that you'll call them if you know you won't be calling them. They might feel hurt and deceived. It is best just to say, "I had a great time tonight" and leave it at that. If you do want to see them again, don't play games and don't leave it a couple of days to contact them. If you don't contact them within a couple of days, it will seem as though you couldn't be bothered, or that you didn't enjoy the date. The sooner you tell them what a great time you had, the better, as they'll really appreciate this. You'll also know where you stand. Also, the man should ask the woman to let him know that she got home safely, as this shows that they care, even if they don't see that person again.

16. HOW MANY PEOPLE CHEAT ON THEIR PARTNERS WITH SOMEONE THEY MET ONLINE?

"Cheating is like spitting on the soul." This is one description I have heard describing the pain and hurt that cheating caused that particular person. Let's be honest, it's not nice to be cheated on.

I've often seen people on the train swiping right or left on their phones, so it's fairly obvious they were using a dating app. Many of these people had wedding rings on, so there's no doubt that some were going home to their partners. Modern technology allows more people to connect than ever before, but this also has drawbacks, as it enables people to conduct extramarital affairs, both physical and emotional.

Some people enter the world of online dating because they are bored and want to try something different. Many people have affairs because they're looking for instant fun and an ego boost. Online dating provides the platform for all of the above to be found with just one swipe right with your index finger, but finding out that your partner is having an affair is horrible and not something that anyone should experience.

The advance of technology has created more opportunities for people to cheat on their partners. Online communication can lead to people becoming intimate more quickly. It's easy for people to get lost and caught up in the world of online dating, which is much more ambiguous and less inhibited. Like-minded people looking for an escape from the constraints and routine of the real world can share information that they otherwise might not feel comfortable sharing.

Recent statistics on infidelity show that around one in three married people have admitted cheating on their partners in one form or another. A 2016 study by the Associated Press and the *Journal of Marital and Family Therapy* showed that 22% of men admitted to cheating on their significant other at least once during their marriage and that 14% of wives admitted to straying. Statistics also show that around 10% of affairs begin online, while around 40% of affairs that start online turn into real-life affairs.

Be with someone who ruins your lipstick, not your mascara!

In the rat-race of a world we all live in today, people are always "on the go" due to work, family and social/peer pressures. Life isn't easy and online dating is an escape from the real world. It's actually healthy to talk and interact with different people, much like a counselling session for people who suffer from anxiety or depression. For lots of people, it's a chance to get lost in this different world for a short period of time and escape from normality. For some people, serial daters, for example, this is all they want, so if you're looking for a long-term relationship you should tread very carefully. It can be difficult to avoid these types of people, as they don't always tell you the truth.

There are many reasons why cheating occurs. Usually, it's because one or both partners are unhappy, but cheating can occur through pure curiosity, because the couple have grown apart, because someone is being neglected, because their sex life has become boring or non-existent, or because they've fallen out of love and are staying together for the sake of their children. None of the above is a good situation for anyone to be in, so before you get to that stage you should sit down with your partner and talk to each other about the issues you have, to see if you can work through them. If you can't, then it's much better to end your relationship and be with somebody else when you've got a clear conscience. This way no one ends up getting hurt through cheating.

Modern technology has created a constant temptation due to its ease-of-use, popularity, secrecy and prevalence. People can connect with old flames through Facebook or Twitter and they can flirt with co-workers over e-mail.

Maybe worst of all, there are also now apps and websites dedicated to helping spouses cheat. Apps such as Hide My Calls and Hide My Texts give people the ability to hide communications received from specific contacts. There are also websites tailormade for this purpose, such as Ashley Madison, which is an online dating service for married people who are looking to stray.

MAIN REASONS PEOPLE CHEAT ON THEIR PARTNERS

1) 77% – lack of love
2) 74% – want more sexual partners
3) 70% – neglected by current partner
4) 70% – drunk, or not thinking clearly
5) 57% – boost their own self-esteem
6) 43% – anger
7) 41% – feeling unattached

In addition to this, a third of the people questioned admitted that they cheated purely because they wanted to have sex.
Source: *The Journal of Sex Research*

17. THE THREE DATING TYPES – LOVERS, LONERS & SERIAL DATERS

There are lots of people out there who are not happy just being with the one person, so how can you tell if the person you are meeting is genuine or if they are a serial dater?

In the complex and bizarre world of romance that exists today, maybe best described as the "hook-up culture", there are three types of people: the "lovers", the "loners" and, of course, the "serial daters".

The "lover" is a hopeless romantic who longs for an everlasting and loving relationship with their soulmate. They will stay involved with "the one" for months and months, or even years and years, without a second thought. They need consistent companions and manipulate their lives so almost every aspect of their well-being revolves around the other person. They do not like being single and they crave companionship.

The "loner" is very independent. "Independent" is perhaps a friendlier term than "loner". They don't believe in relationships because their work and social lives are far too busy. They are far too good to be involved with someone else while they're working hard towards their career. These are the people who might go on a date every few weeks, but who believe the right person will walk into their lives when they're not looking and when they least expect it. They are comfortable with being single and with whom they've become and they don't feel the need to search too hard for someone to date.

Lastly, there is the "serial dater". The serial dater is the most dangerous out of the three dating types. They are witty, charming and romantic one moment, but they'll be a totally different person the next day. Serial daters require social approval, covet material riches and often focus on earning money, showing off success, or dating someone who can bring them such rewards. Whilst focusing on these priorities, they try to avoid the emotional entanglements that come with intimate relationships, perhaps because they have been hurt in the past. This stops them from "letting people in", something which the lovers are more than happy to do.

The serial dater is hard to read and will change their mind regularly. They will leave you shocked and hurt when you find out that they're also doing exactly the same things with other people. The way they talk to you may also change from one day to the next, being very warm and affectionate one day, then very distant the next.

They are chatting or messaging several different people at the same time and they move quite easily from one potential partner to the next, almost instantaneously. You might be left shocked and hurt when you realise how quickly their emotions can change and how quickly they can drop you. You were an urge that they had at the time, their pick of the day, maybe even their flavour of the week. They hate the thought of being alone or having no attention. However, you might be a serial dater yourself and so open to the constant flow of new sexual experiences in your life.

18. DATING PERSONALITY TEST

It is important to understand that everyone is different and everyone has a different personality. You won't get on with everyone you talk to and you will have many highs and lows when trying to find what you are looking for. Have you ever wondered what type of dating personality you have and which dating type you would come under? Are you a lover, loner or serial dater? Whilst this test should be treated as a bit of fun and might not be 100% accurate, your answers should reveal which of these three dating types you are most similar to. The answers are at the bottom.

1) What would you say is most important to you?
a) Love
b) Money
c) Sex

2) What are you looking for?
a) Long-term relationship
b) Go with the flow and see what happens until I meet someone I really like
c) Hook-ups

3) How do you feel about being single?
a) I hate being on my own
b) I don't mind but the right person will walk into my life
c) I love having "me" time

4) How do you dress on a first date?
a) Clothes you think will impress him/her
b) Wear something comfortable and casual
c) Whatever you feel like wearing

5) How long do you need to decide whether you will go on a date?
a) A few days
b) A few weeks
c) A few hours

If most of your answers were As, you are more likely to be a LOVER, which means you are romantic and looking to find the love of your life to settle down with. If most of your answers were Bs, you are more likely to be a LONER, which means that not only are you used to being single, but that you're also content with being single and independent and that you believe the right person will come into your life when the time is right. If most of your answers were Cs, you are more likely to be a SERIAL DATER, which means you are looking for a casual relationship and probably not ready to settle down with anyone just yet.

19. DATING AN OLDER PERSON

There have been many examples throughout the ages of couples who have had a large age difference between them. You cannot help who you are attracted to or who you fall in love with and love does not discriminate. The sayings – "age is just a number", "you're only as young as you feel" (some people also say, "you're only as old as the person that you're feeling") and "as long as you're happy" – all apply, as they are all true.

However, according to a study conducted by Emory University in Atlanta, Georgia, the bigger the age difference, the bigger the chance of separation. After analysing 3,000 people, it found that couples with a five-year age gap are 18% more likely to split up than couples of the same age. Interestingly, that figure rose to 39% for couples with a 10-year age gap and a shocking 95% for those with a 20-year age gap.

One famous example of a couple with a large age gap are the actors Harrison Ford and Calista Flockhart; the age gap between them is 22 years. George and Amal Clooney are another power couple with a large age gap who have enjoyed a fruitful marriage since 2014. Even though George Clooney is 17 years older than Amal, it has certainly not stopped them from embracing a passionate relationship. They married in Venice, Italy, when George was 53 and Amal was 36.

Emmanuel Macron, 40, the President of France, is married to Brigitte Trogneux, who is 65, an age gap of 25 years. Macron recently spoke out about the international obsession with the age difference between himself and his wife.

"If I was 20 years older than my wife, nobody would think for a single second that we couldn't be legitimately together," he told *Le Parisien*. "It's because she is 20 years older than me that a lot of people say, 'this relationship can't be tenable, it can't be possible.'"

> I wake up smiling every morning. I think it's your fault.

In all relationships you'll have ups and downs and, inevitably, the first thing anyone will point to if things go wrong is the age gap.

It really does depend on what stage of your life you're at and what you're ultimately looking for. If you're a man and you want children, you won't want to date a woman older than 50, for example. If you're in your 30s and you date someone in their early 20s, they are at a completely different stage of life and it's likely that they won't want to settle down but will want to experience having fun and having regular "girlie" or "lads" holidays, something that you will probably have already done. It's likely that person will not be as mentally mature as you are.

If you both already have children, you are more likely to be more settled in your lives. Therefore, the older you become, the more the priorities in your life should become much clearer.

Why would a man want to date an older woman (also known as a "cougar")? Well, older women are often more mature and financially independent. They can also be better lovers and they usually won't mess with your head too much. There are real benefits for a man dating an older woman. A lot of the time, men complain that women don't know what they want and that they're high-maintenance. If you try dating an older woman, she is more likely to appreciate some of the different things a man has to offer. These are just some of the positive aspects of dating an older woman.

If a man in his mid-twenties dates a woman in her early or mid-thirties, it is likely he will go through an enriching life-changing experience. While the average twenty-year-old woman is likely to be energetic, ambitious and a go-getter, a woman in her thirties has lived a little more and has learned the world isn't all it was cracked up to be. She will be more settled and less likely to want to go clubbing every weekend or spend money she hasn't got.

In exchange for peace of mind, you have to be willing to accept some of the implications that may come with dating an older woman. More often than not, the advantages overwhelmingly surpass the drawbacks.

It is still very common, almost clichéd, to see an older man with a much younger woman. There is still a long way to go before the idea of a woman dating a man much younger than her becomes fully accepted in society.

For a woman, there's something romantic, alluring and even reassuring about dating a man who's quite a bit older than her. These men tend to be way more settled, trustworthy, well-established and courteous. They tend to be chivalrous, romantic and more old-fashioned.

Older men are usually more focused, straightforward and assertive and will tell it how it is. They act with intention because they usually have a busy lifestyle with great jobs and hobbies that they're passionate about. They've spent enough time in the world of dating to know exactly what they like and want, and they know what turns them off as well.

In dating an older man, there is more stability, and more than simply a chance of a future together and for long-term commitment. Older men are more likely to have a stable mind and this is exactly what makes them so focused in pursuing their significant other. That can make them equally as intentional and focused when it comes to planning for and talking about a serious relationship and its future.

> Life without love isn't really living, it's more existing.

An older man–younger woman relationship can work wonders for women who are looking for men who will not stray, who are calm, thoughtful and stable. When a younger woman finds the right older man for her, these are great foundations that are already laid in her quest to find the perfect soulmate. Younger women who are drawn to older men can bring a lot of youth and energy to the relationship. Often, younger women are more adventurous, spontaneous and romantic, and are more likely to spring surprises and do things on the spur of the moment, which is perfect for the romantic and "old school" older man, who knows exactly how to wine, dine and court his lady, but also wants to break up the routine and be surprised every now and then. Young women are usually more mature than their male counterparts of the same age.

Usually, you will know where you stand when dating an older man or woman because someone older is less likely to have the time and inclination to play games. An older man or woman can be foundational in helping someone younger discover more about themselves. If they both fall in love, they can build a life together that's based on mutual love and respect.

20. CATFISHING

On the whole, online dating is a fun and exciting world where you are able to meet someone new without having to leave your bed or sofa. However, as our lives become increasingly social media-dependent, there is a darker side of online dating that is growing rapidly.

Do you really know the person who is behind the social media and online dating profiles? There are people out there who lie about who they are and it can be extremely difficult to know if someone is being deceptive or not. Such a person is known as a "catfish", and "catfishing" is the term used when someone creates a fake profile on dating apps or on social media sites to trick people into thinking they are somebody else.

One report has found that romance scam victims in the United States and Canada lost nearly USD $1 billion between 2015 and 2018. It is estimated there may be more than one million victims of romance scams in the United States.

The biggest indication that you're chatting to a catfish is their unwillingness to meet you in real life, someone who keeps coming up with lame excuses as to why they can't meet you.

They make up a different life story and use photographs of unsuspecting victims to create fake identities. Catfishers add life experiences, jobs, hobbies, friends and photographs to their fake accounts.

The TV programme, Catfish, has inspired me to tell everyone I'm not the same as my pics. I'm way hotter in person!

Where did the term "catfish" come from? The term was first used in the 2010 US documentary, *Catfish*, in which Nev Schulman tells the story of how he discovered the gorgeous young woman that he fell in love with online was actually a middle-aged, married mum. Schulman fell in love with Megan, but also spoke to her mum, Angela, half-sister, Abby and stepdad, Vince, online.

At the end of the documentary, Schulman revealed that "Megan" was a fake account run by Angela using a family friend's photos. After becoming suspicious, Schulman drove to the address where "Megan" lived and found and confronted Angela, who admitted she was behind the account all along.

Nev Schulman was tricked into falling in love with a fake persona. Afterwards, he told a story about how live cod were shipped along with catfish to keep the cod active and ensure the quality of the fish. He uses the metaphor to describe Angela, saying there are always "catfish" in our lives who keep us alert, active and on our toes. Schulman later turned the documentary into the *Catfish* TV show, where he helps others solve their online relationship mysteries.

There are two types of victims: 1) the people who are duped into trusting someone with a false identity, and, 2) those who have their personal photos stolen, which are then used by someone that is not them.

Not everyone using online dating sites is looking for love. Scammers create fake online profiles using photos of other people. These scammers even steal pictures of real military personnel. They profess their love quickly and they tug at your heartstrings with made-up stories about how they need money for emergencies, hospital bills, to help sick family members, or travel. They do this because they're ultimately looking to steal your money.

Furthermore, romance scammers are now involving their victims in online bank fraud. This is how it works: a romance scammer will set up a fake dating profile to meet potential victims. After they form a "relationship" online, they come up with reasons to ask their love interest to set up a new bank account. The scammers transfer stolen money into their victim's new account and then tell their victims to wire the money out of the country. Victims think they're just helping out their soulmate, never realising they're actually aiding and abetting a serious crime.

WARNING SIGNS THAT AN ONLINE LOVE INTEREST MIGHT BE A FAKE

1) If the scammer asks you to swap numbers and chat offline immediately, without you having built up any connection with them – but you fall in love with their pictures.
2) If the scammer asks for your personal information – don't discuss with them anything to do with money, where you live, or where you work.

One thing you can do, if you think you might be chatting to a scammer, is to carry out an image search of any photo, using your favourite search engine. If you've done an image search and that person's photo appears under several different names, you're most likely dealing with a scammer. If the person's online profile disappears after a few days of you meeting them, that's another sign they are probably not really who they say they are.

21. CASUAL RELATIONSHIPS

Not everyone who uses an online dating app is looking for love or a long-term relationship. You may just be looking for fun, for something physical, or for something short term. If you are, there are plenty of options available, just at the end of your fingertips. You may not have the time for a long-term relationship (LTR) or you may not want one because you've just come out of one.

Many people have casual sex, which can be very exciting and give you a real buzz but, equally, it can be very risky too. You need to take the same precautions as you would when meeting anyone online, but it's even more risky, as you will be ending up in bed with this person at the end of the night (they are a complete stranger!).

Don't get too drunk and don't leave your drinks unattended at any stage. Keep an eye on your drink when the bartender serves it, especially if your date goes to the bar and, if you go to the toilet, make sure you have finished your current drink so there's no chance of it getting spiked. It's really horrifying to contemplate, but **"date rape"** is becoming more common.

Sexual assault is any type of sexual activity that a person does not consent to. Date rape drugs are illegal and are sometimes used to assist a sexual assault. Both men and women can be drugged and the drugs can cause you to be confused or even to pass out, so that you cannot consent to sex.

If you do end up back at your date's house, keep your phone nearby. It's always best practice to let someone know where you're going and who you're going with.

Make sure you **also practise safe sex and use contraception**. The male should always wear a condom. The last thing you want is kids with this person, as a result of what could be a one-night stand! Also, you don't want to contract an STD (sexually transmitted disease)!

If you're sleeping with someone on date number one and you're both only after casual sex, there's a greater risk of you contracting an STD. If you're sleeping with someone this quickly then it's highly likely that you both have frequent sex buddies.

The rise of online dating has correlated with another more disturbing trend. STD rates are also very much on the rise. In a recent study in the US, health officials linked recent STD outbreaks to the rise in Internet dating. Although it wasn't proven to be the main reason, it is hard to ignore the similar pattern upsurge.

Some of the best research on the sex lives of dating app users indicates that dating app users tend to have more sexual partners than non-app users. This means that people who are drawn to online dating apps may be more sexually active than non-users. According to lead study author, Justin Lehmiller, who is a sex and psychology researcher with Ball State University, "It may not be that the technology is increasing the risk, but rather there's this selection effect for people who are more sexually active who tend to use the apps." To summarise, what matters more to users than the apps themselves may be the behaviour of the other people who use them. In any case, dating apps and sites appear to be helping facilitate connections – and disease outbreaks – that might not have otherwise happened.

A previous study found that, in general, women regret one-night stands more than men. However, a new study has revealed that young women regret casual sex less if they take the initiative and the sex was good.

Researchers interviewed 547 Norwegian and 216 American university students, all of them heterosexual. They found that women feel less regret if the "partner was skilled and they felt sexually satisfied". All participants in the study, which was undertaken by researchers at the Norwegian University of Science and Technology (NTNU) and the University of Texas, were under 30 years old.

The findings are a reminder of the importance of a woman's ability to make autonomous decisions regarding sexual behaviours. The women in the study have a healthy sexual psychology and are seemingly extremely comfortable and clear with their own sexuality. Also, women who initiate sex have great choice over precisely who they want to have sex with and, due to this, they have less reason to feel regret, since they've made their own choice.

22. DATING SITES & APPS FOR EVERY TYPE OF RELATIONSHIP PREFERENCE & SEXUAL ORIENTATION

Among the thousands of dating apps out there today, there's something for everyone, no matter what your orientation, sexuality, kink, or relationship preferences. Whether you're straight, bisexual, gay, lesbian, or transsexual, whether you're into bondage, fetishes, threesomes or swinging, or whether you're looking for a cougar or a sugar daddy, it's very easy to find like-minded people in the world of online dating.

Aside from the normal online dating sites and apps out there and the options that they can provide, designers and creators of online dating sites and apps have finally got the message and have delivered great options to cover the vast range of needs, requirements and desires that people have.

People who are looking for a casual relationship are usually much braver online than in person and they're not afraid to get their point across or ask you what you want. This is especially true when it comes to asking about sexual preferences. Women, in particular, are often asked, "Have you had a threesome?", "Would you like a threesome?", "Do you like anal sex?" or "Do you like role play or bondage?" before a proper conversation has even begun. The person asking the question can hide behind their phone or computer without the need to fear a negative response. If you don't like what you hear, you can either block that person or tell them what you think, but it's quite easy for them to move onto the next person and, if they keep putting the same questions to different users, someone will eventually say, "yes".

One common occurrence is the male half of a "polyamorous" couple posting a profile as if he were single.

One good example of this is a date that was arranged where everything seemed normal initially and there was no indication that the male had a partner. It wasn't until he met his date that he explained to her he had a girlfriend, that she had vetted her and that they'd like a **threesome**. A threesome is a sexual activity that involves three people at the same time. This is not what most people are looking for and, in this situation, the male had been deceptive, as he should have been upfront about what he was looking for before he met his date. If you are looking for a threesome or curious about what it would feel like, then just be honest and upfront about it. One popular dating app for people looking for threesomes is Trippple, which has the ability to impress both singles as well as couples who are interested in getting into threesome relationships. There are options for people to meet someone for a casual relationship, or for them to get into a long-term threesome relationship through the connections established through this app.

If you're a younger man seeking an older woman (a cougar), or an older woman seeking a younger man, there are apps like CougarLife.com that allow you to meet, date and fulfil your "MILF" (mother I'd like to f*ck) fetish.

A fetish is classified as a fixation on an object, or a specific situation, that leads to sexual arousal. This also can encompass the obsession someone feels towards physical body parts in a sexual sense. There are new online fetish dating sites popping up on a daily basis.

Grindr is the world's largest social networking app for gay, bi, trans and queer men. Grindr (pronounced "grinder") is a free downloadable smartphone app which finds men who are nearby, as it harnesses GPS tracking, allowing you to establish who else in your direct vicinity is also using Grindr. It shows you – on a gridded display – who these men are and what they look like. It will also tell you how far away they are from you (in feet) and it will allow you to "chat" with them, if you like them. The same safety rules apply as with any online dating app, so it's always best to meet in a public place.

Online dating has been particularly popular with gay men. It's a fact that homosexuality is punishable by death in five countries and parts of two others, according to Grindr's Director of Equality, Jack Harrison-Quintana. He also says, "The fundamental reason dating apps were created in the gay community was to protect users and create a safe environment, no matter where they are located."

For lesbian women, PinkCupid.com is a leading dating site that helps thousands of lesbian singles find their match. As a female-only meeting place, it is one of the most trusted places for women to connect, fall in love and get to know each other. If you're looking for a friend or for the love of your life, you might find them on safe and secure sites such as this. There's a variety of other mobile apps available for sexually adventurous couples and singles looking to find the right partners.

The popular novel, *Fifty Shades of Grey*, really propelled BDSM (bondage and discipline, dominance and submission, and sadism and/or masochism) into the public mainstream. Since its publication, several well-respected newspapers, such as the *New York Times*, have published articles on BDSM.

Bondage is the practice of consensually tying, binding, or restraining a partner for erotic, aesthetic, or somatosensory stimulation. Bondage comes in many forms, and devices used include rope, hog-tie apparatus, whips and chains, hand and feet cuffs, bondage tape, self-adhering bandages, or other physical restraints.

A feather tickler is another device often used for gentle sensory titillation. Although it's often classified as a bondage toy, you don't need to be into BDSM to enjoy being tickled and teased. Lots of couples love using feather ticklers in the bedroom because they don't cause pain, they're easy to use and they feel amazing.

According to a survey by the *Journal of Sexual Medicine*, people who took part in BDSM activities were more comfortable in their relationships than others who chose to play it straight down the line and never experimented.

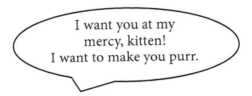

Whether you're into BDSM or you're simply curious about it, there are specific fetish dating apps out there, such as Vanilla-Umbrella. These apps create a conducive atmosphere for singles (and couples) who are into kinky dating to interact with one another, fix dates and even find matches. Apps such as Vanilla-Umbrella have become very useful to those keen on BDSM dating, as the topic still remains taboo in the mainstream.

According to Wikipedia, the term "BDSM" is first recorded in a "Usenet" posting from 1991 and is interpreted as a combination of the abbreviations: B/D (bondage and discipline), D/s (dominance and submission) and S/M (sadism and masochism). The term "BDSM" is now used as a phrase that covers and encompasses a wide range of activities and forms of interpersonal relationships. In general, BDSM communities welcome anyone who has a non-normative streak and who identifies with the BDSM community. This community can include cross-dressers, body modification enthusiasts, rubber fetishists and others.

Bondage and discipline activities and relationships often see the participants taking on roles that are unequal. Usually, one partner is the "dominant" lover, while the other partner is the "submissive" lover. **Consent of both the partners is therefore essential, although there should be consent in any relationship.** The dominant partner ("dom") takes psychological control over the submissive ("sub") and the terms "top" and "bottom" are also used. The "top" is the instigator of an action, while the "bottom" is the receiver of the action. There is a subtle difference between the terms: "Dom/Sub" and "Top/Bottom". One example is someone who chooses to act as the "bottom" by being whipped, but purely recreationally and because they like it, without any implication of being psychologically dominated. An example of the flexibility between these terms is of a submissive who may be ordered to massage their dominant partner. Despite the "bottom" (the "sub") performing the action and the "top" receiving, they have not necessarily switched roles.

You may have heard of female-specific titles, such as "mistress", "domme" or "dominatrix", that are used to describe a dominant woman, instead of the gender-neutral term "dom". A dominatrix is usually a female sex worker who dominates others for pay. Individuals who can change between top/dominant and bottom/submissive roles – whether from relationship to relationship or within a given relationship – are known as "switches". Two switches together may negotiate and exchange roles several times in a session. The precise definition of roles and self-identification is a common subject of debate within the BDSM community.

BDSM is becoming increasingly popular, according to one recent survey, with 64% of men and 51% of women responding they would either like to "be tied up" or "do the tying" (from a sample size of 600,000 people).

Some dating sites have also reported that daters have been expressing a growing interest in bondage and rough sex over the past few years. There has been a huge spike on Valentine's Day, in particular, which is the same weekend that the three "Fifty Shades" films were released in cinemas and theatres. Is this purely a coincidence?

23. IT'S ALL IN THE KISS

It is often said that "it's all in the kiss". Come the end of the night, you should know if you want to kiss your date, or sense whether they want to kiss you. If there is a strong connection between you both, you may even lean in for a kiss earlier than that. Many thoughts go through your head when you're on a date and especially when you're about to leave each other to go home (or not, as the case may be). Just don't force anything!

When it comes to kissing, these questions will have gone through everyone's mind at one point or another, depending on the situation. Do I make the first move to kiss my date? Do I ask if I can kiss them? Do I kiss them on one cheek or both cheeks? Do I put my arms around them? Do I pull them closer? Do I kiss them on the lips? Should I use my tongue? Where do I put my hands? Do I invite them back to mine for a tea or coffee? Do I offer them a lift home? Do I walk them to the station? Do I invite them to stay at mine?

These are all common questions which you would usually only decide at the time and it helps to have confidence in your actions and in how you ask a question. Inviting a date back for a tea or coffee, or giving them the option to sleep at your house, can be dangerous, as it's likely to only lead to one thing. Do tread carefully here, as it's also very forward. Is this what you want on the first date? Often, if you sleep with someone on the first date, you won't last long term as a couple and it can ruin things going forward. Alcohol also often plays a part in this decision and it can confuse a situation; so whilst it's good sometimes to have a bit of Dutch courage, it's better to drink in moderation. Especially on a first date!

With kissing, if you're too shy, this might put the other person off, but equally, they may look at it favourably. If you're too cocky and arrogant it won't normally go down well. A happy medium is the best way to be. I think it's better for a man to pluck up the courage and be brave, as a woman sometimes prefers a man to be a man in this intimate and potentially awkward situation.

> If you love someone, tell them. Hearts are often broken by words left unspoken.

You can tell a lot from the other person's body language. If they are happy and you've been touchy-feely or holding their hand for some of the night, then a kiss is definitely on the cards. However, some women don't want a kiss to be forced. Often, a peck on the cheek (or both cheeks) is what your date would prefer and it can be awkward if you move in to kiss them on the lips and they turn their face and offer you their cheek. On other occasions, you will both move closer together in unison and your lips will lock together like fridge magnets. Every situation is different and every person is different, but don't be too empowering or over-confident. If you're a man, be charming and be a gentleman. Lean towards your date and say that you've had a nice evening. Usually, you can tell at the time whether your date would prefer a kiss on the cheek or the lips. Sometimes, you would prefer not to kiss someone at all, or to only kiss your date on the cheek.

Kissing arouses our senses like nothing else. It activates all five senses and sends a direct signal to the part of our brain that is associated with love, lust and passion.

This exchange of sensory information provides non-verbal clues about the person we are kissing, such as their genetics, overall health, compatibility and level of commitment. These clues affect how attracted we feel and help us to make a subconscious decision as to whether or not we want to go home immediately, go for round two, or pursue a relationship.

As in all great relationships, a great kiss is about connection and compatibility and requires more than just chemistry. We are programmed to like people who are similar to us and who make us feel safe, understood and comfortable. Whether it's your first kiss or you've been together for years, it's this compatibility that helps make a kiss truly memorable.

You can usually tell a lot by a kiss. It's a powerful chemical signal that runs through your body and you should usually be able to tell immediately whether you like someone or not. If there's not much lip or tongue motion, or you have to take the lead with your goodnight kiss, they may be inexperienced, quite shy, or perhaps they don't want to be there. If it's a passionate kiss, they clearly like you. If you like someone you'll want to see them again and, even if the kiss wasn't great first time around, you'll want to try again – so don't give up!

Just remember this one piece of great advice: **you don't owe anyone a goodbye kiss!**

24. PUBLIC DISPLAYS OF AFFECTION (PDA)

Public displays of affection (also known as PDA) is the term used to describe any form of physical contact between couples in a public place. This term covers everything from kissing and cuddling to holding hands or exchanging light touches, such as touching your date's knee.

Any PDA usually depends on where you are at the time, who you are with and who can see you. The question should always be: "Is it appropriate or not?" For example, holding hands in public is seen as romantic and inoffensive. But, if you're sticking your tongue down your date's throat, it may offend certain people, so there's a time and place for everything and you should be respectful.

If you're meeting someone offline for the first time your expectations are usually high, but it's not unusual to suffer disappointment, as they may not quite meet those expectations. If they do and you're getting on well, most people appreciate some sort of light physical contact from their love interest. As humans, it ultimately comes down to a need for physical interaction between two people, which is intrinsic to human nature. Some people are more affectionate than others, but in general, guys need PDA more at the beginning of a relationship and women need it more through the duration of a relationship. However, relationship roles trump gender roles.

Reading the signs is very important. You don't want to lean in for a kiss and have your date turn their cheek on you. That would be embarrassing and could lead to a very awkward "rest of date". At the beginning, especially on a first date, when you're not that familiar with someone or haven't reached that level of comfort, everything you do is considered either a bold move or a serious risk. With that risk always comes the chance of rejection, but embracing your vulnerability will ultimately lead to your greatest confidence. If you're both singing from the same hymn sheet and you've read the signs well, this is a great start!

If you do feel butterflies when you're around the person you like, this is a good sign. Those butterflies will only multiply the moment you hold their hand or touch their skin. Perhaps hold hands with them first and make light touches before you go in for a kiss.

PDA can be seen as confirmation for your date that you are willing to make a love match official. If you hold hands in public, or place your arm around your date, it shows the outside world that you're proud to be with this person and proud to call them your partner.

25. SHOULD I HAVE SEX ON THE FIRST DATE

Having sex on the first date used to be taboo and was seen as a scandal, but there is no right or wrong answer to this controversial question. Nowadays, the unwritten rules of dating etiquette are looser than they have ever been before.

As long as intercourse is consensual, between two adults, then you can do what you like. However, there has to be an element of trust. You are virtually complete strangers, even if you have been chatting online for some time. It's the most intimate thing you can do and it's horrible if you've given your mind, soul and body to someone, only for them to turn around the next day and say they're not interested in seeing you again. You, therefore, need to make sure that you both want the same thing and you have to put an element of trust in each other, but it's difficult to truly know someone if you've only just met.

If you're both only after a casual fling, then it's fine, but if one or both of you is looking for a proper relationship, then I'd say it's best to wait before you have sex with each other. If you make it to date number two, then you know you're both interested in dating each other, rather than just having a "quickie"!

Whatever you decide to do, just remember your decision comes with its own set of benefits and consequences.

REASONS AGAINST HAVING SEX ON THE FIRST DATE

1) If they're sleeping with you on the first date, how many other people are they sleeping with?
2) If you're having sex with someone on the first date, there is a far greater risk of you contracting an STD. Also, in a heterosexual encounter, the female could become

pregnant. Always practise SAFE SEX! Wear a condom, take your pill, do whatever you need to do to stay safe.

3) You want to get to know the person better before you decide on becoming so intimate with them. Sex is the most intimate thing you can do, so you don't want to give them a "freebie" for simply just knowing you. They should have to earn it!

REASONS FOR HAVING SEX ON THE FIRST DATE

1) It's been so long since the last time you had sex and, because you've been away from the dating scene for some time, you find the idea of someone coming on to you just too irresistible.

2) The attraction level and chemistry between you both is so strong that you just can't help yourself. You may have known this person for some time and you may be physically attracted to them, if nothing else.

3) Life is short. You want to live on the edge and have as much excitement as you can, while you can. You are not interested in a proper relationship and you are only looking for something casual.

At the end of the day, whatever experiences you have will influence your future (and your partner's future) in one way or the other. It's up to you what you decide.

26. SEXTING

The term "sexting" was first popularised at the turn of the 21st century and is quite commonly used by people nowadays. According to Wikipedia, the definition of sexting is "sending, receiving, or forwarding sexually explicit messages, photographs or images, primarily between mobile phones", but sexting can be done through any written form of communication, including via e-mail and online dating sites.

Sexting can happen between couples who are already in a relationship, as it can be fun and exciting and can add to a relationship. Sexting also often occurs between two people who have met online – before and after they meet up in person. Sometimes a user will "sext" another user, but they have no intention of ever actually meeting that person face-to-face. For online daters who do meet up on a date, it can make things a little awkward and be embarrassing if they have "sexted" each other beforehand.

There are some "sexters" who look for attention in small doses, but never face-to-face. Some sexters hide behind their phone because they want a quick fix and are only interested in having "sext buddies". Often, this means getting to know someone, well, intimately, without ever actually meeting that person. They would do this by messaging and exchanging naughty messages and pictures. They're usually a completely different person in real life and they usually view the person they're chatting to as a bit of fun and not someone they want to form a relationship with. **Always be wary of sending naked pictures of yourself to a complete stranger, in case they use your photos against you in the future.**

"Is sexting someone you met online, but never met in person, cheating? Is it serious enough to tell my girlfriend? I just feel really guilty."

The simple answer is, "Yes, it is". Your girlfriend or boyfriend probably already senses it. You should be open and tell them. I don't think you would like it if they were doing this to you behind your back. Ask yourself if you would be OK if they did this with other women or men. I think you would feel hurt and betrayed and might think that you're not satisfying them.

27. PHYSICAL APPEARANCES

If anyone says, "It's not about physical appearance, it's about the person inside" they're not telling you the whole truth. Whilst the person inside is extremely important, and probably more important if you want a long-term relationship, you 100% have to like someone physically as well.

I am always suspicious of people who have photos that only show their face, in which they don't smile, if they have only posted one picture on their profile, or if they're wearing sunglasses in every picture. I once met a date who had some teeth missing and I found this really off-putting. Another date was a lot shorter than I was led to believe. I felt deceived and frustrated, as they had lied, and should have told me their true height before we agreed to go on a date.

It's also best to speak to someone on the phone before you meet up, as I've also had instances where I couldn't understand the person because of a language barrier and even because they had a speech impediment. If you don't feel confident talking to someone before you meet up, you could always leave them a voice note using WhatsApp.

Your date might be too small, too tall, too slim, too overweight, too muscly or too curvy. They might look completely different in real life to their photos. You might not like the way they walk or talk, what they wear, or even their hairstyle!

At the end of the day, no matter how many pictures you see of someone, you won't know if you really like that person until you both meet face-to-face. You will be judged too. What you must remember is that physical appearance is subjective. This means that what one person considers physically attractive, another may not.

28. PHEROMONES

Pheromones are invisible and mysterious particles/chemicals in the air which can lead to two people being romantically drawn to one another.

According to Wikipedia, the definition of a pheromone (from Ancient Greek φέρω, phero, "to bear" and hormone, from Ancient Greek ὁρμή, "impetus") is: "a secreted or excreted chemical factor that triggers a social response in members of the same species. Pheromones are chemicals capable of acting like hormones outside the body of the secreting individual, to impact the behaviour of the receiving individuals. There are alarm pheromones, food trail pheromones, sex pheromones, and many others that affect behaviour or physiology."

It might be that you are lured in by someone's pheromones, which are invisible chemical signals that can subtly alter a person's mood, mindset, or behaviour. Some researchers believe that sex pheromones work by sending subconscious signals about your gender to nearby people.

Men who produce higher than average amounts of male pheromones (also known as androstenone) have greater success with women, according to some scientific studies. These are the men that women find irresistible, desirable and seductive and, quite often, they're NOT better looking, more intelligent or more charming than most other guys. They just have an advantage because they produce more pheromones than the average guy.

The effects of pheromones on humans are less obvious than in other mammals, but they still strongly affect our behaviour. Many pheromones are airborne particles that pass through the air after evaporation by the heat in your body. Kissing occurs in all human cultures and this is a way of passing identification pheromones.

28. PHEROMONES

Humans emit what are known as sex scent signals. While it is well-documented that females and males of many species can communicate through chemical signals (pheromones), there has remained some question as to whether humans can communicate this way as well. It also appears that men and women respond to the smells differently.

How effective are pheromones? A group of researchers recently released the findings of a study involving pheromones, conducted on a group of men. According to the results of the study, women are very responsive to androstenone and other male pheromones. In fact, the results showed that 74% of the test subjects experienced a significant increase in the following socio-sexual behaviours: hugging, kissing, and sexual intercourse.

29. DEMANDING PEOPLE & MATCHES THAT DON'T TALK

Why is it that some people you've just matched with don't answer a question, or don't ask you any questions in return? Several times in the past I've written to someone I've matched with and composed an introductory message, ending it with, "How are you?" or "How's your week going?". Often, the response has been a basic "Hi" or "I'm fine, thanks" and they haven't even bothered asking a question back. Why does that person even bother matching with you in the first place if they're not really interested in talking? Some people are very strange!

Some users actually state in their profile that they won't give a response to anyone who asks, "How are you?" as they consider this to be a boring and unoriginal question. I do agree that you should write more than just this, although you can still get the same lack of response when asking this at the end of a long introductory message. It might be a repetitive and boring question, but you're also being polite and it's a nice thing to ask. It does make you wonder if these people are serial daters fed up with being asked the same question or if they want to get down to talking dirty as soon as possible. Maybe they're far too fussy and are never going to settle. Maybe they would prefer a cheesy chat-up line instead? Personally, I always avoid the person who says, "Don't ask me 'How are you?'".

If you don't like somebody's picture, just swipe left. Don't match with someone and then not talk to them as it's pointless and really rude.

I don't get why some people who you match with don't then engage in a conversation. If you initiate a conversation with a match, say hello to them and ask them a question. Why do some people answer your question but then not ask you a question in return? If I ever come across someone who doesn't engage in a conversation, it's an immediate red flag for me and I won't reply to them as they haven't asked me anything about myself. They're either clearly not interested (in which case, why did they swipe right?), someone who seeks a lot of attention but doesn't reciprocate, or they could be very boring. Plus, if they can't engage in an initial conversation online and want to get to know you, what chance would you have if you met them in real life?! I wouldn't want to find out, to be honest, no matter how much I liked someone physically. My advice would be to avoid such people, as you want someone to show an interest in you too.

> Once you feel avoided by someone, never disturb them again.

Very often you talk to someone for quite a while before you meet them, but you still won't know what they're really like until you get to know them better and in person. It's only after a few dates that you start to see someone's true colours and learn what they're really like as a person. Many people have insecurities, some more than others. They often cover up their insecurities with a very confident, brash and narrow-minded approach.

You should also be aware of control freaks as well as narrow-minded, demanding and false people. One user wrote, "I won't date anyone if they don't have a great first-class degree." A classic response to this was, "Is that really important to you then? I'm clever and have a good job, but I don't have to justify myself. I believe you should like the person for who they are and not for what they have written down on a piece of paper. If someone hasn't been to university, it might be because they couldn't afford it, or because they wanted to go to work instead, as they were more practical than academic. I've met some real idiots who have all the qualifications in the world. Maybe you need to open up how you think? Clearly, that's the be-all and end-all for you, which I find is quite sad really. It's a very clear-cut, narrow-minded and clinical view, but you're entitled to your own opinion. I'm just a bit more open-minded, thoughtful and adaptable than that."

Some people may never settle down. There are lots of online daters who are high-maintenance and people can be very materialistic, which is not attractive at all. If someone is too opinionated, they are likely to be too much hard work. It's fine to know what you want, but if someone always thinks they are right, or they are too argumentative and they question you often, it's time to move on to the next person.

30. WHEN IS THE RIGHT TIME TO CALL SOMEONE BY A "PET NAME"?

This is a personal thing and everyone has different views on this. How soon is too soon to start using pet names with someone? Just like Marmite, some people love them and some people hate them. Some people believe that pet names should not be used until you are officially going out with someone, whilst others use pet names on a regular basis as a sign of affection.

Some people don't like being called a pet name, such as "honey", "babe" or "sweetheart", but in certain parts of the world, that's how people talk if they're chatting to someone they like. I have often heard people say, "Please don't call me that!". Statistics show that most people don't like being called a pet name initially, when you have just started talking to them. However, most people don't mind being called a pet name once they have built up a connection or relationship with someone.

That being said, you should be able to be yourself around your date and feel comfortable with them, but certainly not feel on edge. If you're an affectionate person and often use pet names but you're worried that your date will pick up on pet names that you call them, it's really not a good start, so you might find that perhaps you're not suited to each other.

31. CHEESY CHAT-UP LINES

You have just matched with a gorgeous girl or a handsome guy that you fancy and you want to grab their attention with a great first message. Many people would send a generic message, like "How are you?" or "Nice to match with you. How are you today?" These are very common questions and they don't take a lot of thought or effort.

If you want to stand out from other users, you really need to say more than this. You could send a funny, cheesy chat-up line or maybe a joke that will hopefully make your match laugh. A good joke, if written properly, can get a reply from the person you've matched with. Everyone likes someone who has a good sense of humour and using humour is also a good icebreaker.

Cheesy chat-up lines aren't necessarily bad, although some people take a dim view of them. There is no way of you knowing this beforehand so you would be taking a risk. If you do it properly, you can really grab someone's attention in a positive way.

Tradition dictates that men should make the first move when it comes to dating, but with dating apps such as Bumble, where women have to make the first move, out there now and in a world where equality is the way forward, this old tradition is slowly changing. However, many women still feel nervous about breaking the status quo and still believe in the old tradition, but many other women have more confidence these days and are happy to make the first move.

SOME CLASSIC CHEESY CHAT-UP LINES

If I said you had a beautiful body, would you hold it against me?

Thinking of you keeps me awake. Dreaming of you keeps me asleep. Being with you keeps me alive.

Your eyes remind me of spanners. Every time I look at them my nuts tighten.

Do you have a plaster? Because I just scraped my knee falling for you.

You want to know who I'm in love with? Please read the **first word** again.

Do you have a map? It's just that I'm getting lost in your eyes!

Excuse me, is your name Earl Grey? Because you look like a hot-tea!

You have great legs! What time do they open?

I'm not an organ donor, but I'd be happy to give you my heart.

Are you a parking ticket? It's just that you've got "fine" written all over you.

32. HOW MANY PEOPLE "TIE THE KNOT" WITH SOMEONE THEY HAVE MET ONLINE?

Online dating can be a scary place at times. In truth, you're really meeting a complete stranger, so it's always best to meet in a public place. Yet ONLINE DATING IS NOW THE MOST POPULAR WAY SPOUSES-TO-BE MEET. As time goes by and more happy couples decide to tie the knot, the percentage of married couples who met by swiping right is likely to increase significantly. Sociological scientists have seen a trend of heterosexual couples who meet online and pop the question quickly. One study has concluded that couples who meet online tend to get hitched much sooner than couples who meet offline. Dating apps have fast-tracked marriages, as people meeting online know they are meeting someone who wants the same thing. When two compatible people meet and have lots in common, there is no reason for things to go slowly.

TOP 2017 TRENDS IN MARRIAGE PROPOSALS

In 2017, 19% of brides in the US (1 in 5) reported meeting their significant other online. Of this 19% of brides, 17% met through online dating and 2% met through social media outlets. For the couples who met through an online dating app/website, this was a total increase of 3%, up from 14% in 2015. Other popular ways that couples met include through friends (17%), college (15%) and work (12%). This rise in digital dependence continues through each step of the wedding planning journey, with 9 in 10 couples using mobile devices for wedding planning activities in 2016.

The source for the above statistics is The Knot, the leading online wedding brand, and figures are based on The Knot's recently released results of *The Knot 2017 Jewelry & Engagement Study*. Their biannual comprehensive report, the largest of its kind, surveyed more than 14,000 engaged or recently married brides and grooms from the US to uncover the trends and financial spending habits of proposals in America.

'Tis better to have loved and
lost than never to have loved at all.
Alfred, Lord Tennyson

33. ONLINE DATING FOR SINGLE PARENTS

Being a single parent can be tough and can make dating very tricky. This is especially true if you have young children. However, being a single parent does not mean that you have to be single forever.

Online dating is a minefield, but as a single parent, it can feel tougher than for people who don't have kids. Not everyone wants kids, or wants to date someone with kids, and your self-belief and confidence can suffer and be very low at times. It takes some people a long time to get over the stigma of being a single parent – especially when it comes to dating.

What you should understand is that being a single parent is something to cherish and celebrate and you should never forget that. The right person for you will also recognise this and will work with you, as they'll know that you won't have too much free time. Flexibility is the key.

Your kids will always come first, and rightly so, as you'll always be protective of your kids. It's best not to give out too much information about your kids to a new online connection. Don't tell them where you live, where your kids go to school, or anything that's too personal. At this stage, they don't need to know anything else other than you have kids, how many kids you have and maybe how old they are. Initially, it should be about you getting to know an individual better, and vice versa.

Online dating has made it much easier for single parents to meet new people. EHarmony is one dating app which helps you connect with other single mums and dads out there. There are other sites, such as SingleWithKids.co.uk, which have been created with the specific aim of matching single parents who are in the same boat. You should be honest with people that you're a parent, just as you should be honest about anything you put on your profile.

Dating can be costly and also time-consuming. Money and time are more valuable to a single mum or dad than to someone who has no children. To most single people, a date costs a few drinks and maybe a meal, but they don't have to factor in the extra cost of a babysitter, so a date night for a single parent takes a lot more effort and, usually, there are extra costs involved.

Apart from having more choice, the main benefit of online communication for a single mum or dad means they can chat to an online acquaintance when their kids are in bed, or when their kids are playing and they're sitting on the sofa. This means they don't have to devote and commit to a whole night out. To meet someone face-to-face is a big commitment and single parents don't want to be wasting their time.

There are other dilemmas to consider as well. Does the person that you're chatting to have kids themselves? Do they want kids? Do you want more kids? What are you/they looking for? It is important that both of you are singing from the same hymn sheet.

Once you have been dating someone for a while, provided that you like each other and can see a future together, you will then think, when is the best time to introduce them to my kids? If you both have kids, you would need to discuss whether you are both happy for all the kids to meet each other. This is a huge decision, so don't rush into making it. Many people are wary about introducing a new partner into a child's life, in case things quickly go wrong with the relationship. It's not good if a child sees many different partners coming and going in their mum or dad's life. They won't have any sense of security and could be hurt if they never see a person again, with whom they've built up a level of trust and with whom they've had a good relationship.

Many people fear dating once they have had kids and they lose confidence, as they know they can't devote the same time and energy to meeting someone in the same way they did before they became parents. They may also be hurting from the breakdown of and fallout from a previous relationship and this can also put someone off from searching for love again.

You should be open that you are a parent and you should NEVER apologise for this. Be proud that you are a single parent and, if someone is terrified about the prospect of taking on children, there is no point in spending time with that person.

Every person is different and every situation is different, but everyone deserves true happiness. You should always remember that there is someone out there for everyone. With the help of online dating apps, you can meet good people and you will hopefully meet your soulmate. Stay positive and don't give up on your dreams.

34. "CUFFING" SEASON

The cold nights draw in, the sunlight disappears and the days shorten. You're single, unattached and you just want someone to snuggle up with and keep you warm during those long, cold and lonely evenings. Welcome to "Cuffing" season.

This is the modern term used to describe the period during the fall/autumn and winter months in which lonely singletons find themselves seeking to be "cuffed" or "tied down" by a serious relationship. You would be forgiven for thinking that "cuffing" is a kinky term and something to do with BDSM.

Online dating apps, such as Tinder and Bumble, see a big increase in the number of active users and sign-ups during the months of November through to February. Cuffing season usually kicks off on 1st November and runs until the day after Valentine's Day (14th February). During this period, people who would normally prefer to be single or promiscuous find themselves (along with many other singletons) wanting to be cuffed. The cold weather and forced indoor activity cause singletons to become lonely, so many look for someone to spend this time with. Christmas can also be a lonely time of the year for people who are not in a relationship.

Cuffing is often viewed as being temporary and seasonal. It can be this, yes, but it can also lead to a serious long-term relationship. Put simply, it's the act of finding a significant other for the sole purpose of staying warm during the cold winter months. Although cuffing season tends to be casual and fun on the whole, we all know that relationships aren't usually as simple as that. Feelings can develop, even if the initial goal is to just have a cuff buddy over those colder months. If feelings are mutual, you need to talk to your cuff buddy and you should always go with your gut instinct.

Serious relationships can occur and develop when you least expect them to. Emotions can quickly change and there's always the possibility of falling in love with a new online acquaintance. Once you've matched with a prospective partner online, you will need to evaluate whether or not they are looking for the same thing as you.

"A good cuffing partner is one that makes plans in advance, instead of just asking you out for the upcoming weekend," says Dr Jane Greer, a New York-based relationship expert. Someone who plans in advance shows signs of commitment, which is a great indicator for a long-term relationship.

Being attentive is also very important during cuffing season and there is no reason for either of you to play games and be distant with each other. When your cuff buddy messages you, you should reply as soon as possible. You should be available to hang out with your cuff buddy at least once a week, that's if you want to keep them around until the spring. You may have been hanging out together and doing cute, fun and sexy things whenever you meet up, but unless you have both agreed that you want to be on each other's social media, you probably shouldn't be adding any couple pictures just yet. You should remember that this relationship is most likely going to end come springtime, so flaunting it online might not be the best idea at this stage. You're having great times together now, but come those warmer months, you should not assume you will be invited to any family gatherings or parties.

Over time, scientific studies have proven that cuddling releases the happiness hormone, oxytocin. Once this hormone is released, it is human nature to continue doing the same thing that caused it to be released. This is simply because it makes us feel good and makes us happy. Cuddling up with a cuff buddy on those long winter nights is obviously going to lead to some fun and sexy times, but, as we all know, if you're having sex you need to be responsible and stay safe. Practise safe sex, so that you don't end up with any nasty surprises (or diseases) at the end of cuffing season.

At the end of the day (or at the end of cuffing season) what really matters is that you met someone new and that you had tons of fun with them. Don't take the relationship too seriously at first or look too far ahead. See how things develop with your cuff buddy and go from there.

35. TELLING YOUR DATE THAT YOU'RE NOT INTERESTED & "GHOSTING"

How do you tell someone that you don't want to take things further? For most people, one of the hardest things to do is to figure out how to let someone down and break the bad news that you don't want to see them again. However, it is just part of the dating game, as you're not going to like everyone you meet or chat to. I definitely find it harder if I've actually met someone face-to-face, as I don't like hurting people's feelings, but it does have to be done if you don't feel something for the person you have just met. You have to be honest with that person and also be honest with yourself, or it's just a waste of your time and energy and you will end up unhappy.

An eternal silence, also known as "ghosting", from one person or from both people, is a way of saying that you don't want to see someone again, and this happens often, as it's easier to just ignore people sometimes. It's often easier just to text my date if I didn't feel there was enough chemistry between us. It's much more awkward when you like someone but the feeling is not reciprocated.

Ghosting is now so prevalent in dating culture that we sometimes prepare for it even before we have met someone. Ghosting means that you just disappear (you abruptly stop responding to texts, phone calls, etc.) in the hope that the person you've been dating will get the message and stop contacting you. However, there are other, better, ways to tell someone that you're not interested.

Many people view ghosting as being disrespectful and cowardly, and it's not nice to be ghosted instead of having an adult conversation or receiving a text message or a message through WhatsApp. It does mean that you build up a thick skin over a period of time.

According to an *Elle.com* survey of 120 women and 65 men, 25.83% of women and 33.33% of men have both "ghosted and been ghosted". Try and be nice to someone, if you can, by respecting the time and feelings of the person you're dating, even when you know it won't lead anywhere.

However, there is an alternative way that you could look at ghosting. In today's society, ghosting is merely the logical conclusion of the generally accepted principle that consent can be withdrawn at any time. If you mix that in with the perfectly reasonable impulse to protect ourselves against the emotional trauma of having to reject someone, or even of being rejected ourselves, this is one way that you can defend the practice of ghosting.

36. DATING IS BECOMING MORE COMPLICATED – MODERN DATING TERMINOLOGY

Modern dating can be tough and complicated. If you are searching for love, finding someone who is willing to commit to you and won't stray is tough enough, but even finding the time to fit dating into your own busy, hectic lifestyle can be difficult. Sometimes it feels as though everyone else has a manual to follow, so hopefully this book will go some way to providing you with a greater insight into the world of dating.

Online dating has sometimes been compared to a game of cat and mouse, with many people constantly on the prowl looking for love or looking for the next best thing. As the world grows smaller and people have become/are becoming more connected, social media only perpetuates our anxieties and this can create added pressures. However, even with all of the pressures we face in modern society today, it is important to remember that dating should also be fun!

With one in four of us now finding love online, a completely new language for modern dating has been created. It feels like a new dating term or trend is being created every week.

We've just talked about ghosting, where people don't have the civility to end things verbally or by text. They ghost the person they've been dating, which means they ignore them with no explanation. This is just one of the many new dating terms people use nowadays.

Here are fourteen new digital dating behaviours that you should be aware of:

1) GHOSTING

Getting over a break-up can be really tough, regardless of whether it was a long-term or short-term relationship. Ghosting means that you don't hear from that person again. They disappear forever like a ghost and they will cut off all communication completely. You can end up driving yourself crazy wondering what you did wrong and questioning why you did not hear from that person again.

2) ZOMBIEING

Zombieing is another popular new dating term. It's where you've been ghosted for a while and then, from out of nowhere, your ghoster gets back in touch. The person you were dating disappears, then comes "back from the dead" months later, with some lame excuse to justify their prolonged absence. They are most likely to get in contact with you again through a social media platform or through an out-of-the-blue text message. Usually, the zombieing happens just when you've gotten over the hurt of having them ghost you in the first place. Then, all of a sudden, they subtly reappear, causing more emotional upset.

3) SUBMARINING

This is when you stop seeing someone because they ghosted you and they have cut off all communication. They then reappear after some time and act like nothing ever happened. This is similar to zombieing, but submarining is actually worse – after resurfacing, they'll offer no explanation, acknowledgement or excuse whatsoever for their disappearance. Basically, it's when someone you've been seeing or talking to vanishes without a trace (much like a submarine when it sinks to the depths of the ocean), then, without warning, they resurface and slide back into your inbox like nothing ever happened. People who submarine you either want to hide the reasons for disappearing or they just want to gloss over it.

4) STASHING

Stashing is the latest dishonest dating technique that you may have been a victim of. It occurs when the person you're dating doesn't introduce you to their friends or family and doesn't post about you on social media. Basically, you're their secret boyfriend or girlfriend, who they feel justified in stashing in the corner, pretending nothing is going on to the outside world and keeping their options open. Stashers don't want a loving relationship with you and will be chatting to and seeing other people.

5) BREADCRUMBING

Breadcrumbing is when you send out flirty but non-committal messages (breadcrumbs) to a person, but you're not really interested in dating them. You send the messages in order to lure a sexual partner without expending too much effort, which equates to leading someone on. If you've been dating someone, breadcrumbing can also mean you don't have the guts to break things off with them completely, as the breadcrumber doesn't like confrontation.

6) CUSHIONING

This term refers to someone with a new partner keeping several dating options on the backburner – just in case their main relationship goes wrong. If the person you are with is acting suspiciously and being very secretive – especially with their phone – they could be cushioning.

7) FLEXTING

Flexting is when you boast online to impress your date before you meet them in real life. According to data from PlentyOfFish, 47% of single people have experienced this, via a person who brags to them over texts to big themselves up. It's usually women on the receiving end of this behaviour, with 63% of women reporting having received messages like this, compared to just 38% of men.

8) CRICKETING

This has nothing to do with a bat, ball and village green! "Cricketing someone" is when you deliberately leave a text message on "read" for too long. In some cases, it can take days or even weeks for the other person to reply and continue the conversation. Instead of getting a response, the sender is met with a deafening silence. Cue the crickets. The majority of single people, 67% of them, have said they've waited patiently for a reply and have received one way later than expected. Are they too busy or not that interested?

9) GHOSTBUSTING

This is a word for the people who don't give up. Ghostbusting is where you continue to text someone when they are continually ignoring you (ghosting). According to PlentyOfFish, 78% of single millennials have been ghosted by someone they were dating! Of all the people surveyed, 38% reported being in a situation someone wouldn't stop texting them after they tried to phase them out. Personally, I wouldn't bother! Why waste your time with someone who clearly doesn't like you enough?! You should just turn the tables and block them!

10) SERENDIPIDATING

Serendipidating means that you leave things up to fate and put off a date just in case someone else comes along who you like more. As there is so much choice, you could be missing out on "The One" by being too dismissive, too soon. Nearly a third of singles said they believe the grass is always greener and have admitted to putting off a day and time to meet for a date, just on the off-chance they meet someone in the interim. There has to be a limit, though, as otherwise you'll be swiping forever – alone.

11) FAUXBAE'ING

Fauxbae'ing is a curious habit that 19% of single men have witnessed. It's when someone pretends to have a significant other over social media when they're actually single. So, effectively, they are lying and it's probably a tactic to make an ex jealous or an attempt to make nosey family members leave you alone. Either way, it's quite sad that they have to stoop to this level.

12) BAE

You may have heard people using the word "bae" and wondered to yourself, what does it mean? Well... bae is a slang term often used nowadays to refer to a boyfriend, girlfriend, lover, crush, or romantic online connection. The trend is particularly popular amongst teens and young adults, who tend to use it as an alternative to "babe" or "boo" on social media, or via text and WhatsApp. People who use "bae" tend to replace someone's name with it or they will omit the word "my" when referring to their significant other. For example, instead of posting a status update that reads: "Hanging out with Lisa" or "Hanging out with my boyfriend", you would instead say: "Hanging out with bae".

13) SAPIOSEXUAL

This is a new term which is popping up more regularly on user's dating profiles. It means that your perception of someone's intelligence is one of the most important factors in your attraction to them. It's one of the new ways to self-identify on OkCupid and is basically someone who is more drawn to the specifics of a partner's mind than the specifics of a partner's body. If you find a person physically attractive, but they seem stupid and unintelligent, you would lose all sense of attraction to them if you were a sapiosexual. If someone is not so physically or otherwise attractive, but they seem smart and clever, there's a good chance that a sapiosexual would be turned on. Being attracted to someone in this way has been described as feeling like "foreplay for the mind".

14) ORBITING

This term is taking ghosting further. Sometimes, the same person who ghosted you will keep watching all of your Instagram and Snapchat stories. They will retweet your tweets and even leave the odd "haha" comment on your photos. This is all while ignoring your direct texts and messages. They can carry on doing this for months, or even years. It's really odd behaviour and is also very rude too. Anna Iovine, who coined this phrase, explained the trend is so called because the person doing the orbiting is keeping you "close enough that you see each other, but far enough to never talk". If you've been ruthlessly ghosted, it's really frustrating (even more frustrating than being ghosted – which you wouldn't actually think was possible). You should delete someone that has been ghosting you, so they can't orbit you as well.

Trying to keep up with new terminology can be confusing and mind-boggling, but many of these online acronyms and abbreviations are now officially part of the English language and can be found in Oxford Dictionaries.

37. ONLINE DATING FOR TEENS & YOUNG ADULTS

Recent statistics tell us that online dating usage among young people has significantly increased over the past few years.

Many young adults at college have access to college-specific online dating sites. One in five (20%) of all Harvard students have used a college-specific site, as well as 50% of Columbia University and New York University students.

According to research carried out by eHarmony, online dating usage among young adults (18–24-year-olds) has tripled since 2013. In 2013, 10% of this age group reported using online dating. In 2018, this figure rose to 27%. This is largely due to the introduction and subsequent growth of mobile dating apps, but it's also down to the development and increased usage of the smartphone in our pocket.

Young people are more likely to meet someone online, as opposed to in a bar, and if you consider that only 9% of women and 2% of men find relationships in a bar, your chances of finding someone online are far greater. There is also far greater choice online.

Staying safe online is imperative for everyone – possibly even more so for teens and young adults. There are many predators and catfishers out there who will try and lure you in. Parents and teachers have a big role to play in keeping children safe. By building up a child's digital resilience, parents will not only help keep their child safe online, but essentially empower them to navigate digital issues on their own.

During your teenage years, it's natural to be curious and you may start to become interested in dating. Sometimes you might not be ready to start dating, but you feel pressure from your peers that you have to, just because everyone else around you has started. Some parents of teens will be very restrictive about the age their children can start to date, but this can lead to teens dating in secret. Before you start dating it's important to think about a number of things, and we're going to take a look at five of the most common now.

1) PEER PRESSURE ON TEENS & YOUNG ADULTS TO DATE

Has everyone else in your peer group started to date? If they have, you may feel pressured into dating as well, for no other reason than that everyone else is doing it. However, if you don't feel ready to date, it could make you feel uncomfortable and unhappy. You should try and avoid dating someone until you feel comfortable in doing so and until you meet someone that you really like. True friends will understand and won't try to put any undue pressure on you. If you are being pressured, it may be time to stop seeing your current friends and surround yourself with people who allow you to be yourself and are happy for you, whatever decisions you make. You should try and talk to one of your parents or to another responsible adult that you can trust, to seek their advice.

2) MEDIA INFLUENCE ON TEENS & YOUNG ADULTS DATING

Most television programmes aimed at teens, such as *Love Island* and other reality TV shows, feature numerous young couples having fun. If you're a teen, it can be hard to watch these programmes and still feel like you shouldn't yet be dating, especially if all your friends have started to pair up because of the influence these programmes have. Popular media often portrays teen dating as being normal and can give a false impression of what relationships are really like. Teen magazines and websites can glamorise things and teens can feel under immense pressure from material and sexual ideals. This can lead to unhappiness.

3) THE RISK OF PREGNANCY AND CONTRACTING STDS

Teenagers who are dating may feel pressured into taking part in sexual activities. They may feel that they have to go along with it, and yet they may not be ready or equipped to deal with the consequences. Sexual activity amongst teens can lead to unwanted pregnancies and STDs and no one form of contraception is completely reliable in preventing these. Some STDs have no symptoms, but they can cause severe problems for you in the future. They can lead to infertility, which means that you may not be able to conceive children naturally when you are ready to do so. If you feel like you're ready to have sex, you need to be 100% certain, as it's a big step to take. Ensure that you are both protected appropriately and, if you're female, speak to your doctor about the best form of contraception for you. If you're a male, wear a condom! Even if you are taking other forms of contraception, only condoms can protect against STDs.

4) EMOTIONAL DANGERS FOR TEENS & YOUNG ADULTS WHEN DATING

When teenagers and young adults begin dating, they will start to experience different and intense emotions, particularly if they have been dating the same person for a while. The older you become, the more you change as a person, both physically and mentally. Disagreements, arguments and break-ups can feel like the end of the world for teens in serious relationships and they can lead to feelings of despair, insecurity and inadequacy. In the worst cases, this can lead to teenagers contemplating self-harm or developing eating disorders, so it's important for teens to confide in their parents or another trusted adult to help them get through these difficult times. Parents should keep a close eye on their teenagers, looking out for any signs that they are dating, so they can help them with their emotional roller-coaster ride.

5) OTHER PROBLEMS WITH TEENS & YOUNG ADULTS DATING

Dating can give teenagers and young adults a sense of worth and companionship, but it should not be taken lightly. There are a number of dangers facing those who start dating that did not exist before. Peer pressure from a boyfriend or girlfriend can be even stronger than peer pressure from friends. This could lead to you doing things that you're not comfortable with, not ready for and potentially too young for. You may also feel pressured to dress a certain way, stay out later than you wanted to, pay for things you didn't really want to, smoke, and drink alcohol, all just to try and please your date. If your date is pressuring you to do things that you are not comfortable with or even things which are illegal, you should tell your parents or a trusted adult. You should also question whether they are the right person to be dating.

38. DATING HORROR STORIES

THE GHOST – SOPHIE, 25

I had a nice time on a date recently, but I wasn't overly bothered whether it went anywhere or not. He did seem a lot keener than me. My best friend was encouraging me to see him again and be open to see where it could lead. We had arranged to spend the day together last Sunday. He texted me in the morning to say he had been called into work but was maybe able to meet me later that day and would let me know. I wasn't that bothered, but at 3pm I thought I'd message him to see how he was getting on – no reply! At around 11:30pm I saw he was online, so I messaged him again, asking if everything was alright. He then blocked me on WhatsApp. Very strange!! I had wasted my whole day, as I had planned to be with him. Some people are just crazy!!

THE BLIND DATE – ROB, 34

I had a blind date the other night, but never again! She wasn't what she said she looked like at all. She had short spiky hair, was badly dressed, she didn't smell very nice, had a deep voice and I had to make my excuses after one drink. I paid for the drinks, though, and didn't do a runner, as that's not nice, but I did feel deceived as she lied to me about her appearance!

THE SEX-OBSESSED MAN ON MY HOTEL DATE – ANNA, 41

I met a guy in a hotel lobby in central London. He looked like he did in his pictures, so that was a good start. We had a laugh, we had a few drinks and the conversation was flowing. He then began adding sexual innuendo to everything he said and I didn't realise this at the time, but I was getting drunker by the minute. Later, I realised it was all part of his master plan. At the end of the night, he moved in for a kiss, but it felt very uncomfortable and I didn't fancy him. It was at this point that he dangled his hotel room key in front of me, told me he had booked a room and asked me to come up with him! Even though I was very tipsy, he took me by surprise, made me feel cheap and like a piece of meat! I also feared for my safety, as he was a lot bigger than me and it did make me wonder if my drink had been spiked! It was lucky we were in a public place. I politely told him where to go and went to the reception area and called a taxi. The guy followed me to the reception area and kept on trying his luck, even though I spurned his advances. I couldn't get out of there quick enough and blocked his number as soon as I got into the taxi. I also deleted him from the website I'd met him through. I feel like I had a very lucky escape!

THE FOOT FETISH STALKER — GEORGINA, 36

We met up in the car park of a nice five-star restaurant. After a brief introduction, we went inside and were shown to our table. The waitress took our orders and we talked a bit more. Halfway through our starters, my date went under the table and lifted my legs up with his hands and strategically placed them on his lap, sliding my sandals off first, with my toes pressing against his hard manhood. I said, "What are you doing?" and he said, "I forgot to tell you, I have a foot fetish!" I jokingly said, "Could you not have waited until we'd had dessert to tell me?" mainly because I was in complete shock and I thought that humour would work best in this very awkward situation, in the middle of this five-star restaurant. I took my feet off his lap, but I did finish my main meal. I promptly made my excuses to leave and drove home. He then stalked me online and by phone for a few weeks, even though I sent him a message that same night to say that I wasn't interested in taking things further.

THE BDSM GUY — LILLIE, 33

One guy told me during our first date that he was into BDSM. He said he had been educated at an expensive boarding school, famed for producing some famous people (and perverts!) and he did have a posh voice. I realised after a while that he was more of the latter, but I didn't want to judge him and I had never tried BDSM before, so I was intrigued. After quite a few drinks to calm the nerves, we ended up back at his house, began kissing and we started stripping off. He then asked if he could slip a leather belt around my neck. I nodded "yes", so it was consensual. I allowed him to pull me off the sofa and into his bedroom. It was OK, but I felt more like a keen observer than a sexual plaything. The next day, I had bruises all over my body and teeth marks left in my legs, but I didn't remember being bitten. My neck was sore and I had a mark around it too. I don't think the drinks helped, but I'm glad that I gave it a go for the different experience. I won't be in a hurry to do it again though!

THE REBOUND GUY — CLAIRE, 38

I am a teacher living in London and had been chatting to a guy who lived in Manchester for a couple of months. He was a lawyer and our relationship was growing every day. I developed feelings for this man, but I also knew that he had recently come out of a long-term relationship. There were never any insecure messages from him and he seemed very happy whenever we spoke on the phone. We finally agreed to meet up and he said he had booked a hotel room near to where I lived and had also booked a table at a local restaurant. We agreed that I would meet him there directly. On the day itself, I glammed myself up and made a real effort. We met at the restaurant and he was exactly like I thought he would be. We shared a brief kiss and we were shown to our table. I then got a huge shock as our waiter was a sixth form student that I teach! I was slightly embarrassed, but I said, "Hi," and spoke to him for a couple of minutes. My date and I soon ordered our starters but, unfortunately, our conversation seemed to be all about his recent failed relationship and it was starting to get me down. I decided to nip to the toilet and I then bumped into an old friend, who I spoke to briefly. When I got back to the table, my date was not happy and asked me why I took so long. I explained that I had just bumped into one of my friends, but his mood changed dramatically. A few seconds later, he started crying and said, "I can't do this!" He stood up and flung £40 in notes on the table and walked out. I never heard from him again, but I have never been so embarrassed in my entire life. I began crying myself and was consoled by my pupil and my friend. Luckily, the pupil never said a word to anyone at the school about what happened, but this goes to prove that although you think you might know someone, they can suddenly surprise you.

THE SELFISH DINNER DATE — MATTHEW, 27

I got on really well with a woman online and was excited that we were finally meeting up, as we had been chatting for a couple of months, but hadn't managed to meet up sooner. Looks-wise, she was perfect! We met in a busy train station and I took her to a local restaurant. Bad idea, though, as I soon realised she was quite a selfish person. She didn't stop talking about herself throughout the whole evening. I have never been on a date where they didn't ask me one question! I was instigating all the conversation, but if I hadn't done this it would have been even more awkward. I ended up paying the bill at the end of the meal, but I couldn't eat my food fast enough. I regretted not going for a drink instead, as then I could have left sooner, not felt so uncomfortable and not wasted my time and money. It's amazing how someone can be so different in real life, compared to how you perceive them to be from your conversations online. You are forced to ask each other questions online, as there's no other option when getting to know someone online, but this has taught me that reality can be very different.

39. DATING & DISABILITY

Signing up to an online dating site is a great way of meeting someone, but for many people it's a daunting prospect and having a thick skin is a must. If you have a disability, it can make dating even more difficult, but it should in no way stop you from searching for love online and finding your perfect match. You do, though, have an added dilemma which you need to consider – should you tell someone about your disability up front? Should you make it clear on your profile, or tell your date that you have a disability before you meet them? If you don't say anything about your disability until you meet someone face-to-face, would that be classed as lying to the person because you didn't mention it until then?

If, for example, you're a wheelchair user and you turn up to your first date in your wheelchair, your date is likely to be surprised and possibly annoyed that you didn't mention it to them when you were chatting online. They might feel deceived that you hadn't disclosed your disability to them before you met up in person.

It's always best to be honest and upfront with people – within reason, of course, but people usually want to get an idea of what someone looks like before they meet them. It's similar to the person online that doesn't have any photos or isn't smiling. What are they hiding? Having a disability is nothing to be ashamed of and you will still have all the same dreams and desires as any other person your age, but if you don't tell your date that you have a disability, your date may end up having a lot more questions than they would have done before they knew about your disability. They're not going to know the extent to which your disability affects you and may not understand much about it, so they will be unprepared and it can make things really awkward and uncomfortable for both of you on your date.

Disability naturally comes with added complications; it might be that you need somebody to drop you off, or that you need to have your helper with you. You might have limited mobility, so might not be able to go up stairs and only be able to meet at certain places, which have a ramp. Maybe you have language difficulties that require a certain level of understanding from the other person. It can be overwhelming for some people that you date, as they might not be able to take it all in. They might not be able to deal with the fact that you have a disability, so the more information you can give someone before a date, the better.

You should be prepared for unusual questions. Even if your date knows about your disability beforehand, there are lots of stereotypes attached to different disabilities, so it can mean that people have preconceived ideas about what you will be like.

Unfortunately, you might be asked some strange and maybe even offensive questions. For example, if you have a mobility impairment, you might be asked the very awkward question, "Can you still have sex?".

If your date knew about your disability beforehand, you would be able to let them know if there are certain places or situations that you would prefer to avoid. For example, you might only be able to eat certain foods. If your date reserved a table at a fish restaurant and you didn't eat fish, this would be a problem. If you have a hearing impairment, you might wish to avoid places with lots of ambient noise. Or, if you have an anxiety condition which makes you feel uncomfortable in enclosed spaces, you should propose a date idea where you will be in more of an open space. If you find that you get tired if you're out for a certain amount of time, let your date know in advance that you would prefer to meet up for a few hours, rather than for a whole day or evening.

Over the past few years, online dating has become more accessible for people with disabilities. Online dating websites and apps have gradually become more inclusive over the past few years. This is partly down to the huge growth of the online dating industry.

The main benefit of this is that you now have more choice than ever before. As a disabled person, you might be looking to date another disabled person. In addition, it means that able-bodied people might be more open to the idea of dating someone with a disability. People with disabilities are seen more often on TV, in the media and in society in general. Events such as the Paralympics and the Invictus Games have been so positive in showing the world that, just because you have a disability, doesn't mean that you are any less of a person. There isn't the same stigma attached to dating somebody with a disability as there once was.

There are many niche online dating websites and apps which specifically cater for people with disabilities. Dating4Disabled, designed for use by disabled people only, was founded in 2005. It's a global website with the express aim of bringing disabled people together across forums, blogs and chatrooms. The site tries to create an inclusive atmosphere in which people feel safe to express themselves. It's free to register and its users can share stories and meet like-minded individuals, making the site as much a social network as it is a dating site.

Whispers4u was established in 2002 and connects disabled people from all around the world, with users in countries such as the UK, the USA, Canada, Australia and many European countries. This site also reports on many of the success stories of its users, with pages dedicated to couples who have found love and even got married after initially meeting on the website.

DisabilityDating.com caters exclusively to the disabled community, and sites such as eHarmony and Match.com also accommodate them. They offer specific advice to people with disabilities and those who are open to dating someone with a disability.

At the end of the day, you should want to feel comfortable on your date, so talk things through with your date beforehand. If they are the man or woman of your dreams, they will be understanding and considerate and they will want to know more about your disability, your life and you as a person.

The online dating industry is currently growing by approximately 3.9% each year, meaning that these platforms are set to welcome many more marginalised people from across all walks of life. This will make it an absolute necessity for online dating apps and websites to become even more inclusive, so watch this space...

40. SPEED DATING

This novel concept really became popular around the turn of the 21st century. Speed dating once had an unjustified label as being something that was just for people who were desperate. However, since those early days, it has rapidly become a fun and popular way to meet new people.

Speed dating is a formalised matchmaking process where you get to meet and chat with a number of complete strangers – all of you together in the same room – spending three to four minutes with each person. Once the three to four minutes is up, one of you then moves onto another table to chat with someone else. The time pressure makes it a bit like musical chairs. The woman would normally stay seated, with the man moving from one table to another. To mark the end of your time with each person, a bell is usually rung. You can decide to take it further with anyone that you connect with, but only after you have spoken to everyone (there are usually around 20–30 people in total). You would register and pay for the event online, well in advance of your arrival.

The purpose of speed dating is to encourage people to meet a large number of new people, thereby giving you plenty of choice to find someone with whom you are compatible with. Its origins are credited to Rabbi Yaacov Deyo of Aish HaTorah, and it was initially conceived as a way to help Jewish singles meet and marry.

SpeedDating, as a single word, is a registered trademark of Aish HaTorah. Speed dating, as two separate words, is often used as a generic term for similar events. The first formal speed dating event took place at Peet's Coffee in Beverly Hills, in late 1998.

You need to have confidence to take part in speed dating as it can be very daunting and overwhelming. It's certainly not the place to freeze when meeting someone for the first time. In fact, you meet lots of people for the first time and you're not going to like the majority of those people.

Your words can become repetitive so my advice would be to make sure you take a drink around with you, as your mouth will become very dry!

One of the advantages that speed dating has over online dating in general is that when meeting someone face-to-face, you get a better sense of who they are due to their body language, gestures and tonality, and people are unable to hide behind pictures.

TV shows and films like *Sex and the City* helped glamorise speed dating as being trendy for single young professionals. They also showed that you sometimes need to mix up what you tell people, although it's best not to lie. In one *Sex and the City* episode, lawyer Miranda tells men that she's an air stewardess, after her true profession scared away the first few men she spoke to.

Lock and key parties are less formatted and are more like a regular party than a speed dating event. They are sometimes linked to speed dating events and held at the same venue and at the same time, but in a separate room. Usually, women are given a lock and men are given a key. You then circulate around the room looking for people whose key can open your lock, and vice versa. It's a good icebreaker, as there's definite sexual innuendo involved when a man asks a woman, "Can I see if my key fits in your lock, please?". If you find a match, you both go back to the registration desk. You will both receive raffle tickets or another prize, but it's a great way to get you talking to someone. You'll be issued with a new lock or key, unless you want to spend the rest of the evening with the person you've just met. Lock and key parties suit people who are comfortable in a party situation. You are not guaranteed to meet everyone, but there is a chance to spend more than three to four minutes with people you like and there is more of a relaxed atmosphere than with speed dating. Everyone is supposedly single, so you're all there for the same reason.

Taking speed dating to another level, yoga speed dating now exists. Almost unbelievably, you can now find romance and love when doing the "plank" or downward dog. You can now be at one with yourself – and with other people dressed in Lycra.

Just like normal speed dating, yoga speed dating sees around 40 yogis swap partners throughout the evening, but in a hot, sweaty and intimate setting instead.

You can then practise paired yoga moves, chat with one another, focus on your next move, silently sob, or ask your yoga partner for their number, once the session has finished.

41. WHEN SHOULD YOU DELETE THE DATING APP ON YOUR PHONE, ONCE YOU'VE MET SOMEONE ONLINE?

If you have met someone online and things are going really well between you, at which point do you consider yourself to be in a "relationship" and how long do you wait before you stop using a dating app and delete your dating profile? Is it a mutual decision? Do you both delete your dating profiles at the same time? How long should you wait and how many dates should you have before you make this decision?

Once you start seeing someone regularly, most people will agree that you should wait for as long as it takes before you become "mutually exclusive". It's a conversation that you need to have with your partner and you then need to make a joint decision. There should be no exact parameters as to how long you wait, as it's a decision that you and your partner need to make on your own and you should not be restricted to a certain time frame.

You certainly should not delete your dating profile after two or three dates, as that would be far too early. It's highly likely that you are still chatting to other people at this stage and are yet to make a decision about the person you've just met. You may also be having fun at first and not even thinking about a relationship, but as soon as you both develop feelings and you've had a number of dates, it's then that you should consider becoming mutually exclusive.

You might delete your dating profile because you are happy and don't want to date anyone else, yet your partner is still dating other people, either because they are looking for something different to you or because you have not yet had that conversation which defines your relationship and allows you to express how you feel about you both keeping a dating app on your phone.

Dating apps can easily be downloaded again, but to take an app off your phone is a sign of commitment to your partner – you are letting go of your online presence. It also means that you are giving that person a fair chance and tells them that you are serious in wanting to take things further.

42. PEOPLE WHO ARE QUICK TO JUDGE

One regular question which gets asked when two new online acquaintances start chatting is: "What is your longest relationship?" People who are quick to judge may ask, "What's wrong with you?", just because you might not have dated anyone for as long as they have. If your longest relationship is three years and the other person's lasted 10 years, this can be a problem for some people. To some people, it's a competition and a numbers game, but it is possible to love someone more in six months than you can love someone in 10 years. You could stay with people for longer just for the sake of it, which would increase the number of years spent together. But you won't be happy, so what's the point in doing that?

If things are not right you should try and work things out, but sometimes you can't, and it's unhealthy being with someone when you're both unhappy together. Some people stay with their partner for years and are very unhappy, and this is not healthy. However, if you have children together or share a house, it can make things harder. How do you define a very long-term relationship anyway? Another reason people may not have had a long-term relationship is that they simply just haven't met the right person yet and people should accept that every person's situation, circumstances and experiences are different.

Recent research carried out by dating site, DateWithaMate. com, has discovered that on average, British women decide how they feel about a guy just 1 minute and 30 seconds into a first date. This may sound like a very short period of time, but you will be judged on your physical appearance immediately, as your date will carry out an initial physical survey. In other words, they will size you up! You will also be judged on your personality within those first 90 seconds. Although meeting someone face-to-face makes it easier for you to decide how you feel about your date physically, surprisingly, 41% of women said that in the initial stages, they judged their date on personality alone!

This is in comparison to over half of men admitting to making all of their decisions based on their date's looks/physical appearance alone. Having said that, men are a little more generous than women with their time, as the research discovered that, on average, it takes men five minutes to make up their minds.

One terrible selfie posted online could be the difference between you chatting with someone or not chatting with them, especially if it's your main photo. If you judge someone based on nothing more than their physical appearance, this just encourages shallow and superficial relationships that have no staying power in the long run. This is the result of not having a true interpersonal connection.

If you feel that someone is judging you, it will probably make you feel uncomfortable and like you don't want to take things further with that person. I would also conclude that this person is a perfectionist and perfection doesn't really exist as everyone has their flaws. That person may never be truly happy.

Deciding not to make snap judgements and not to look for instant perfection has to be your goal. You should try to resist the temptation to move on too quickly to the next person at the first sign of imperfection.

Constant competition and the "disposable" nature of online dating naturally takes you into the position of having to be more guarded. However, you should heed the old saying, "Don't judge a book by its cover". You should also not judge someone too quickly, but give people a fair chance.

43. ONLINE DATING FOR OVER-50S

When you reach the age of 50, most of your peers, friends and colleagues will be in stable relationships. If you find yourself single again after coming out of a long-term relationship, you would be forgiven for thinking that your dating options are limited. Equally, if you've been single for a while. But don't stress – there are many options and opportunities out there and online dating can open up a whole new world where you can chat and meet new people and you can also narrow down your search, based on age, location, mutual interests, etc.

Years ago, many people over the age of 50 might have remained single for the rest of their lives, but the surge in popularity of online dating apps has made it easier to find love again, or even to find love for the first time.

It might seem scary and daunting if you're about to use an online dating app for the very first time, but you need to realise that there are many millions of people out there who are in the same boat as you. You should take your time getting to know someone first online, as there are many scammers around, which I've already talked about in my book. If you narrow down your search, there are so many options for you to meet new people whom you would never have met in your normal day-to-day life.

The older you are, the greater the likelihood that you haven't had the same exposure to technology as younger people have had, so navigating your way around a dating app can be tricky at first. Your expectations might also be lower and quite different to singletons in their 20s and 30s. Chances are, people younger than 50 years of age will want something different than you, such as kids and marriage. You may have been married previously and may already have kids of your own.

There's no expiry date when it comes to dating and love. Many over-50s put aside their love lives after divorce, separation or the death of a spouse. However, you CAN find love again. If you've lost a loved one, it will take time for you to grieve, but this doesn't mean that you have to stay single forever. Sometimes it's best just to get back in the saddle. Online dating can help you move on and there are many dating apps that you can use.

> Love has no age, no limit; and no death.

The desire for companionship has led many older adults who are single, divorced or widowed, to sign up for online dating. A Pew study found that from 2013 to 2015, the number of users aged 55–64 years old who dated online doubled from 6% to 12%.

The surge in older online daters has led to many dating apps having a minimum age requirement. OurTime, Stitch, SeniorMatch and SeniorPeopleMeet all require users to be a certain age – usually 50 or 55 – to sign up, creating a more specific dating pool.

Match.com has more over-50s members than any other dating site and it has a simple matching process that is easy to use. SilverSingles and EliteSingles also appeal to and attract relationship-minded singles over 50 with simple, safe, and effective online dating tools.

Recent research by eHarmony predicts that the biggest growth segment in the online dating market over the next decade is going to be the 55–64 age group, who will see a 30% rise in the number of singletons and an increase in their usage of the Internet.

44. ONLINE DATING ABBREVIATIONS & ACRONYMS

In the world of online dating, you will often come across abbreviations and acronyms sprinkled throughout people's profiles. But what do they all mean? There is no manual anywhere, but I want to help you understand them so you aren't left in a state of confusion and so you don't have to suffer the embarrassment of having to ask a friend for help and advice. The numerous abbreviations and acronyms can tell you a lot about an individual, so you really need to know them.

Many online daters indicate their race with an abbreviation. They use W for White, B for Black, A for Asian, NA for Native American and H for Hispanic. Religious affiliation is similarly indicated. For example, C stands for Christian, J stands for Jewish, while LDS stands for Latter Day Saints, or Mormon.

Some online dating abbreviations explain sexual preference. BI means bisexual, and G means gay. Straight individuals will not usually use any special abbreviations to let you know that they are heterosexual.

GSOH means good sense of humour, something that is necessary in any relationship.

Not everyone on a dating site is looking for a long-term relationship, but if you are, then look out for LTR. The opposite is STR, or short-term relationship.

Abbreviations are also used by online daters to let potential matches know what they like in the bedroom. BDSM or SM means that they are looking for some kinky sadomasochistic fun.

Online dating abbreviations are like little clues that need to be deciphered. Your prize for figuring out the puzzle might just be finding the love of your life.

Here is a list of the most commonly used online dating abbreviations and acronyms:

Online Dating Acronyms/Abbreviations	
A: Asian	LS: Light Smoker
AL: Animal Lover	LDR: Long-Distance Relationship
AM: Asian Male	LGBT: Lesbian Gay Bisexual Transgender
A/S/L: Age? Sex? Location?	LOL: Laugh Out Loud OR Lots Of Love
ATM: At The Moment	LSA: Limited Strings Attached (similar to FWB, with perhaps room for change later)
B: Black	LTR: Long-Term Relationship
B4N: Bye For Now	M4M: Man For Man
B&D: Bondage & Domination/Discipline	M4W: Man For Woman
BB: Barebacking	M4MW: Man For Man and Woman
BB: Bodybuilder	M4T: Male For Transsexual/Transvestite
BF: Boyfriend	M: Married
BI: Bisexual	M: Male
BIF: Bisexual Female	MBA: Married But Available
BIM: Bisexual Male	MBC: Married Black Couple
BIMF: Bisexual Married Female	MC: Married Couple

BIMM: Bisexual Married Male	MM: Married Men or Marriage-Minded (be sure to determine which!)
BDSM: Bondage, Discipline, Sadism, and/or Masochism	MILF: Mum I'd Like to F***
BBW: Big Beautiful Women/Woman	MNC: Married, No Children
BHM: Big Handsome/Hunky Man/Men	MOTOS: Member Of The Opposite Sex
C: Christian	MWC: Married With Children
CPL: Couple	MTF: Male To Female (transgender)
CD: Cross-Dresser	MW4M: Man and Woman For Man
CU: See You	MW4W: Man and Woman For Woman
D: Divorced	MWC: Married With Children or Married White Couple
DBF: Divorced Black Female	NBM: Never Been Married
DF: Drug-Free	ND: No Drugs
DDF: Drug- and Disease-Free	NM: Never Married
DILF: Dad I'd Like to F***	NS or N/S: Non-Smoker
DOB: Date Of Birth	NSA: No Strings Attached (i.e. casual/adult relationships)
Dom: Dominant Male	PF: Professional Female
Domme: Dominant Female	PM: Professional Male

D/S: Dominance and Submission	POF: Plenty Of Fish
DTE: Down To Earth	ROFL: Roll On the Floor Laughing
DTR: Define The Relationship	S: Single
DWF: Divorced White Female	SBF: Single Black Female
DWM: Divorced White Male	SBIM: Single Bisexual Male
F: Female	SBM: Single Black Male
FA: Fat Acceptance/ Admirer	SD: Social Drinker
FAQ: Frequently Asked Questions	SGL: Single
F2F: Face-To-Face	SI: Similar Interests
FS: Financially Secure	SM: Sadomasochism
FTA: Fun, Travel, Adventure	SO: Significant Other
FTTB: For The Time Being	SOH: Sense Of Humour
FWB: Friends With Benefits	SOLA: Single Or Living Alone
FYI: For Your Information	SSBBW: Super-Sized Big Beautiful Woman
G: Gay	SSBHM: Super-Sized Big Handsome Man
GBF: Gay Black Female	STR8: Straight
GBM: Gay Black Male	SWF: Single White Female or Straight White Female
GC: Gay Couple	SWM: Single White Male or Straight White Male

GF: Girlfriend or Gay Female	SWS: Sex Without Strings
GSOH: Good Sense Of Humour	T4M: Transgendered looking For Men
GTG: Got To Go	TDH: Tall Dark and Handsome
GTSY: Good To See You	TG: Transgendered
GWC: Gay White Couple	TLC: Tender Loving Care
GWM: Gay White Male	TS: Transsexual
H: Hispanic	TV: Transvestite
HIG: How's It Going?	TYVM: Thank You Very Much
HAK: Hugs And Kisses	VBD: Very Bad Date
IMO: In My Opinion	VGL: Very Good Looking
ISO: In Search Of	W: Widowed or White
J: Jewish	W4M: Woman For Man
K: Kids	W4W: Woman For Woman
N/K: No Kids	W/E: Well-Endowed (yeah – right!)
L: Lesbian	WLTM: Would Like To Meet
LD: Light Drinker	WTR: Willing To Relocate
LF: Latin Female	YO: Years Old

45. REVIEW OF SEVEN OF THE MOST POPULAR DATING APPS

Which dating app should I choose? Which apps are for romance and which are for casual fun? Where will I find everlasting love? Where will I bag myself a bedroom playmate? How much will it cost? Which app has the most choice? Which app is easiest to use?

These are all questions that people regularly ask, so to help you with your decision I have reviewed seven of the most popular dating apps so you can see what each of them have to offer. Hopefully it will help you to decide which app is most suitable for you.

TINDER

People first started using Tinder in September 2012. Since then, it has probably become the most popular and most famous dating app out there. It is used by tens of millions of people each month. Tinder users swipe 1.6 billion times each day and the app is used in 196 different countries, worldwide. Tinder has significantly helped remove some of the stigma of online dating.

As of June 2018, Tinder had 3.5 million users. Users originally needed a Facebook profile to be able to use the app, with Tinder profiles being built using Facebook information. However, in July 2017, an alternate sign-up was made available. Match group (which owns Tinder) stressed that Tinder profiles were now largely user-generated and that matching algorithms did not rely on Facebook or any other third-party data.

When Tinder first exploded onto the scene, it was used more as a hook-up/no strings sex app, because it finds you potential matches based on people's proximity to you and based on you swiping right on someone's main profile picture, and vice versa. Now, almost everyone seems to have the app downloaded on their phone, but it's not just used for hook-ups these days. I have many friends who are in long-term relationships with someone they met on Tinder. I also know people who have married the person they first met on Tinder.

Tinder offers a simple way to meet people online, as it's very easy to use, as well as free. You can sign up through your Facebook account, to ensure some level of identity verification, but your membership is not posted all over your Facebook account, so your friends and family will not know. You can also sign up outside of Facebook. The app then matches you to other Tinder users who are within your chosen age range and located within your chosen distance range.

There's no real profile creation with Tinder, but you can write a few words in your profile to describe yourself. Photos may be automatically pulled from your Facebook profile pictures. Alternatively, you can click the plus sign on the top right of your profile page to view pictures on your phone, Instagram, or album photos from Facebook, and you can upload any of these photos instead (up to a maximum of six photos are allowed).

Tinder Plus and Tinder Gold are optional additional services, but you have to pay for these. One of the features of Tinder Plus is that it allows you to have Unlimited Likes – you only get a set amount per day on standard Tinder – and it gives you five Super Likes a day, as opposed to the normal one. Tinder Gold costs more but offers you more exclusive features, such as a feature where you "see who likes you" before you decide whether to swipe right on them or not.

It's very quick and easy to join – you simply upload some photos and create an optional bio, set your age and distance preferences, and off you go, swiping left or right on potential suitors. As one of the most popular apps, your pool is likely to be huge and people do actually have conversations on Tinder. In my experience, it's the app where I have had most success and it's definitely not just about sex.

There will soon be a brand-new feature that will shake-up how matches work on Tinder for iOS and Android devices. Tinder is set to roll out one of its biggest changes since the dating app launched. Currently, on Tinder, matches can only message one another once they both swipe right on their prospective date's profile. However, in a future update, Tinder plans to give women the option to choose whether they want to initiate conversations with any future match. The update will mean women have the option to receive messages *only* from men they say they want to talk to. It's a feature that will be very similar to Tinder's rival, Bumble (more on Bumble below), an app where women specifically have to take the first step and initiate conversations with men.

Cost = Free of charge for basic membership in both the UK and US.

Tinder Plus and Tinder Gold are optional, upgradeable services and they give a user more options. UK users have to pay an additional £7.75 per month (12-month package) for Tinder Plus or £11.67 per month (12-month package) for Tinder Gold.

For users in the US, the corresponding figures are approx. $9.99 per month to upgrade to Tinder Plus and then an additional $4.99 per month on top to upgrade to Tinder Gold.

BUMBLE

Bumble was founded in December 2014 by ex-Tinder employee, Whitney Wolfe, who actually sued Tinder for sexual harassment. Bumble is often hailed as the feminist antidote to Tinder's "anything goes" feel. Just like Tinder, both users have to swipe right to match with each other, but unlike Tinder, the first message on Bumble has to be sent by the woman.

What makes Bumble different from other dating apps is the challenges it presents to women to make their move, as men cannot message first. As far as Tinder alternatives go, Bumble is the closest comparison. The user interface is pretty similar in that you upload pictures, put together a little introductory bio and swipe left or right on people's photos. It's very easy to use and some people say that Bumble is better than Tinder, as there's better choice and people on there appear to want something more serious. One thing Bumble allows that Tinder doesn't is that you can send photos in chats – something Tinder users have been waiting years for. Another thing you might enjoy is that women have to take the first step and send the first message. However, this may frustrate you if you're impatient or if you like making the first move.

The idea of Bumble is to save women from receiving creepy advances or cheesy chat-up lines from men. It also takes the pressure off men to start up conversations. However, after you match, you only have 24 hours to start the conversation, otherwise he will disappear forever. Similarly, your match only has 24 hours to reply. If he does reply in time, there is no time limit anymore for future messages. The only problem with this system is that sometimes you're not able to go on Bumble for over 24 hours, so you could miss out on your potential soulmate and lover.

Cost = Free of charge in the UK and the US. However, "Bumble Boost" costs £3.99/$9.99 USD a month. This adds "Beeline", which shows you a list of users who have liked you, "Rematch", which keeps expired matches in a user's queue for 24 additional hours, and "Busy Bee", which allows users unlimited 24-hour extensions for matches.

OKCUPID

OkCupid offers a more personalised approach to free online dating. OkCupid was founded in January 2004 and was a website long before it was an app. It is one of the most popular online dating services of all time. It is more in-depth than most other dating apps and is known for its incredibly long profile requirements, although you do upload photos too, as you would do on any other dating app. The whole point of the app is to make your profile as thorough and descriptive as possible and to create a percentile score for users that reflects your compatibility with others. You are even asked to answer supplemental questions about things like music, movies, politics, life, religion, sex and education, plus you can list the six things you couldn't live without, the first things people notice about you, what you're really good at, etc., which will help find even more precise matches.

You are able to like other users and message them directly, but messaging is the better option of the two, as users can only see who has liked them if they have upgraded to "A-list" status.

Cost = Free of charge in the UK.

In the US, the cost is $14.95 for one month, $29.85 for three months, or $47.70 for six months.

MATCH.COM

Match.com is one of the oldest dating sites around – it was created way back in 1995. It has remained at the top of the online dating world since long before its official mobile app was released.

If you're taking dating seriously and looking for a relationship, I would recommend Match.com, as it's an app which has an excellent website offering its members a comprehensive suite of services. These include a massive user base (and access to said user base), personalised daily matches, excellent matchmaking algorithms and more. However, it will cost you a membership fee in order to gain access to everything, whereas a lot of the other apps I have reviewed are free of charge. There are free trial periods, but if you're trying to take advantage of everything that Match.com has to offer, you will need to pay.

One added benefit of Match.com is that users can browse for same-sex relationships. Regardless of relationship preference, there is no way to know what type of relationship someone is looking for, whether casual or serious, unless they specifically state it in their profile.

Cost = In the UK: £29.99 a month, £19.99 a month for three months, or £9.99 a month if you choose a six-month subscription.

In the US: Generally, a one-month subscription costs around $31.99; a three-month subscription costs about $17.99 per month for "standard" or $20.99 for "value", and a six-month subscription runs about $15.99 per month (standard) or $18.99 per month (value). Match.com offers a guarantee that if you don't find someone in six months, you will receive another six months for free.

PLENTYOFFISH (POF)

PlentyOfFish is not as easy to use in places as some other dating sites, but it is modified frequently, new features appear regularly and members are matched not only on what they say they're looking for, but also on the pattern of their browsing for potential daters.

POF is a popular and frequently visited site. The more users there are, the more chance you have of finding your perfect match. PlentyOfFish tells you how many people are online at the time – rarely is this number under 500,000 – and will break it down further into "My Matches", "My City", and other categories. However, because it's free to use, I did find that most people I spoke to were after a casual relationship rather than a long-term relationship. You can upgrade in a few different ways to a paid membership, but this is one of the best free online dating sites.

PlentyOfFish works by matching you with those users who you are most compatible with and this is done by asking you to take their special POF Relationship Chemistry Predictor test. This measures self-confidence, openness, family-orientation, self-control and social dependency. It's a great site if you want free access to a large database of single people.

Cost = Free of charge in the UK.

While technically a free site in the US, PlentyOfFish offers you the option to purchase a membership upgrade. Upgrading costs $35.40 for three months, $51.00 for six months, or $81.40 for one year.

EHARMONY

Founded in August 2000, eHarmony is one of the oldest dating sites around and is still very popular. It takes a scientific approach to finding love and matches singletons based on key dimensions of compatibility, which have proven over time to be the foundation for a long-term relationship. It analyses traits such as character, intellect, morals and values.

Exclusively built for users seeking long-term relationships, eHarmony stipulates that subscribers must be single, widowed, or divorced – separated individuals are not allowed to set up a profile, which is a bit strange! While the eHarmony site allows only for opposite-sex matching, there is a companion site called Compatible Partners, which is for those seeking a long-term same-sex relationship.

If you are serious about searching for love and initially want to look deeper than pictures alone, this could be the site for you. EHarmony has even patented "The eHarmony Compatibility Matching System". After years of research, they have come up with a Relationship Questionnaire and pride themselves on this scientific approach and on matching users with people who are compatible with each other and who they think will have matching personalities. EHarmony provides quality over quantity and is a great app for those looking for a long-term relationship.

Cost = In the UK: £9.95 per month.

In the US: $59.95 for one month, $39.95 per month for a three-month subscription, $29.95 per month for six months, and $19.95 per month for 12 months.

ZOOSK

Zoosk was founded in December 2007, so has been around for quite a while. The romantic dating app found its feet through Facebook, initially, and is now one of the biggest dating apps in the world. It is heavily integrated with social networks and smartphones so you can access the app via many different platforms. It helps users find romance online and has a multitude of members from around the globe enjoying the service each month.

Zoosk has been one of the top online dating sites for many years and has a very logical approach to online dating. It is different to other sites in that it uses a matchmaking engine, which monitors your behaviour on the site, to help narrow down your dating pool. Zoosk is also known for its "gamification" of the dating process, where members can use coins (a virtual currency) to buy gifts for other users and boost their profile so more users can see you for a limited period of time. Zoosk has about 33 million profiles from single people in 80 different countries and is available in around 25 different languages.

Cost = Free members can browse, wink, and respond to e-mails they receive; they cannot initiate e-mails. However, upgrading to premium status allows you to chat and send e-mails to any other members.

In the UK: For full membership, the cost is £11.99 per month (based on you taking out their six-month package).

In the US: Premium status costs $29.95 for one month, $19.95 per month for a three-month subscription, or $9.99 per month for a full year.

46. LONG-DISTANCE RELATIONSHIPS

You cannot help who you fall in love with, but staying in love is another thing entirely and it's even harder to do if you're in a long-distance relationship. Most online dating sites and apps allow you to set a distance radius on your profile, which will only show you all potential suitors within that particular radius. This, of course, creates greater choice but also means there's a greater chance of you meeting someone who lives far away. If you choose to use an app that doesn't have this service, or you decide to increase the distance radius on your profile, you might start chatting to other users who live hundreds of miles away, or even to users living in different countries. If you get on well with someone online, there's a chance you will begin a relationship with that person, so in this instance, it would be classed as a long-distance relationship (LDR) at the start, simply because of where you both live.

Not being able to see someone regularly can be tough. Added to that, if you embark on an LDR, you have to consider the costly phone calls, expensive plane tickets, time differences, etc. That said, many of us end up having a long-distance relationship at some point, for the simple reason that love is not always rational. When you are in love, the feeling is rare and very powerful, so there should be no barriers to love.

LDRs can work and *do* work and, thanks to advancements in technology, you are able to FaceTime or Skype someone even if you're living on opposite sides of the world. However, this is no replacement for physical contact, so you have to really want your relationship to work and ensure that you speak to, message and FaceTime each other regularly. An LDR can take its toll, but you try to tough it out for the sake of love, even when it's difficult. Usually, when people see each other again, the intimacy and sex are amazing.

The other main key to maintaining an LDR is trust. You must not stray whilst apart, otherwise the feelings will diminish and your relationship will peter out. Stay faithful and make sure you stay in regular touch with one other.

The ultimate goal is for you both to leave behind your long-distance love story and unite in the same city. This should always be the main objective that you are both working towards and you should never lose sight of this.

47. CONCLUSION

The world of online dating can be fun and exciting, but can also be complex and confusing. The key is to persevere and to keep trying. Never give up! It's often said that love and the right person will come along when you least expect it. Everyone deserves happiness, but for some people it can take longer to find than others.

Have respect for others and never be rude to anyone. Even if you've had a bad date, put it down to experience and try to forget about it. It happens to all of us and everyone you speak to will be able to tell you a tale of at least one horror date they've experienced.

It's important to understand that the main purpose of online dating is to create a platform that enables you to chat with people before eventually meeting them for face-to-face dating.

Remembering this main objective will prevent you from getting sidetracked and drawn into the limitations of dating online. After getting to know someone for a while, it's best to move a connection toward an actual date, otherwise you can end up just becoming pen pals and putting people in the friend zone. People you talk to just become a fantasy, as you're never going to meet them in person, which really defeats the main purpose of online dating.

If you're overwhelmed by having access to too much choice, you need to find a way to narrow down your searches and find better matches. Often, people match with another user and never talk to them, which is pretty pointless, really, so try and be more selective and only swipe right on someone whose pictures AND profile you actually really like.

If you get frustrated with talking to someone online (which should be the case after weeks and weeks of talking without actually meeting up), then suggest a meeting in person. Just don't leave it too long. If you follow that process, it will be much easier to find that magical connection, both online and face-to-face, which almost everyone is looking for.

Ask yourself if you are enjoying your match's company and enjoying their conversation. If the answer is "no", you should move on to the next person. Your match should be wondering if YOU like THEM and they should be attentive and show great interest in you. **You are the prize, so always remember that.**

Don't go out with someone just for the sake of it and certainly don't settle for second best. I have come across many people who have done this. They have dated – and even married – the first person that came along. You must make sure they are the right person for you and be selective. Feeling those butterflies and having that connection with someone is vitally important.

If you're looking for love, you will hopefully find the man or woman of your dreams online and will share many years of happiness together. If you follow the guidelines and advice in my book, the result will be that you achieve a healthier, happier and more successful dating life.

47. CONCLUSION

The key is to trust your instincts and get to know more about someone online first, before moving on to the next stage and meeting them in person. Have fun with the process, but also be cautious.

Stay safe, be honest and have respect for others. Always remain positive, as you will need a thick skin at times, but have fun and enjoy your online dating adventures.

Printed in Great Britain
by Amazon